The Life of Mary Revisited

Being an Abridgment of
THE MYSTICAL CITY OF GOD

By
Ven. Mary of Agreda

Abridged by
Sister Mary Frances Hilbert, OSM

From the English Translation of
Rev. George J. Blatter (Fiscar Marison) 1912

The Life of Mary Revisited

ISBN No. 0-9758593-0-7

Publisher's Note:

On August 15, 1999 upon starting to write this abridgment of *City of God*, Sister Mary Frances wrote to the proper authorities about copyright rules and received a reply on September 1, 1999 that the four volume set is in the public domain.

Sister has faithfully abridged "The Life of Mary Revisited" from this four volume English translation by Fiscar Marison.

Publisher:

W. P. Reynolds
355 Dover Road
Westwood, Mass. 02090

CITY OF GOD

An abridgment of the translation
done by Rev. George J. Blatter
who wrote under the name Fiscar Marison

In the seventeenth century a Spanish nun was chosen
to write the divine history and life of Mary, the Mother
of God. She was Sister Mary of Jesus, a cloistered Franciscan nun living in Agreda, Spain.

In order to do this special spiritual assignment, she was
gifted with many visions of various kinds. Among her
spiritual favors was the grace of bilocation, which transported her to the southwestern part of our country, the
area which now contains the States of New Mexico and
Arizona.

She was a member of a most extraordinary family. Her
mother and her younger sister entered religious life, and
her father with two of his sons also entered the Order of
St. Francis.

Sister Mary of Jesus did her writing as an act of obedience, a virtue which she called great, "not only because
by it the most noble activities in the faculties of a creature, namely the mind, the judgment and free will, are
offered as a holocaust to the Lord; but also because no
other virtue ever assures success more unfailingly than
obedience."

These revelations show the great esteem the Queen
of Heaven has for this virtue of obedience, and for the
virtue of humility which is its companion.

This is a very brief introduction to what will follow.

Our Lady of Sorrows Convent
Feast of the Immaculate Heart of Mary
June 12, 1999

FOREWORD

Life is a mystery and those closest to the hearts of Jesus and Mary are dreamers. It is heavenly to know that dreams can come true.

After high school graduation, I lived a very worldly life for six years. During that time, I met a girl who told me about a Novena held every Friday evening at St. Mary Magdalene Church in downtown Omaha. In answer to my prayers, I met a wonderful Catholic young man who seemed to have all the qualities I would like in a husband.

One evening he called to say he wanted me to see the film "Bells of St. Mary's." I really did not want to, but he insisted. I told him we could go to the Novena service first, then have dinner and watch the movie. As he knelt beside me in church, I prayed, "God, if You want me to marry him, please make me love him very much, and if You don't, please take this love for him out of my heart."

As we were watching the scene of the Sister praying so fervently in the chapel, my heart said, "That's what I really want." Being that close to Jesus was my deep desire.

As I continued attending the Novena services every Friday evening, I suddenly noticed what one sentence was saying, "Make me worthy of the title Servant of Mary." A few weeks later, I entered the convent and loved every part of religious life as it was at that time.

One day while I had some extra free time, I went to the convent library and found a very old book with the title CITY OF GOD. This was a brief presentation of Ven.

Mary of Agreda's revelations, and almost every chapter had instructions from the Blessed Virgin Mary telling how a woman religious should practice her virtues to draw closer to perfection. This book seemed so holy that I felt I should kneel while reading it. I made little notes which I carried in my pocket and read them frequently, hoping to grow in holiness.

A few years later, I had a Silver Jubilee celebration and received a small amount of money to purchase WORDS OF WISDOM. This was a collection of Our Lady's instructions contained in the writings of Ven. Mary of Agreda. It was approved for me by a Jesuit spiritual director.

Later, in a different situation, it was possible for me to receive the complete four volumes which I read many times. The other books about Mary, which I had read, seemed to be earth looking up to heaven; CITY OF GOD was like heaven looking down to earth.

A few years later during a retreat, I had the inspiration to write an abridgment of these volumes. I do owe much gratitude to those persons who have given me encouragement and partnership, Mr. William Reynolds and my Prioress Provincial, Sister Jean Morrow, O.S.M.

Feast of the Annunciation of the Lord
March 25, 2004

CITY OF GOD

Written in four Volumes

I. THE CONCEPTION

The Sacramental Mysteries wrought by the Most High in the Queen of Heaven from the time of her Immaculate Conception until the Incarnation of the Word in her virginal womb, and how much merit she herself acquired through divine grace by profiting from the favors conferred upon her during those first fifteen years of her life.

II. THE INCARNATION

The Mysteries of the Life of the Holy Mother of God from the Incarnation of the Divine Word in her virginal womb to the return of the Holy Family from Egypt.

III. THE TRANSFIXION

The Sacramental Mysteries of the Life of the Mother of God from the return out of Egypt up to her Divine Son's Ascension into Heaven.

IV. THE CORONATION

The heavenly Life of the Queen of Heaven, most holy Mary, containing the events of her life from the Coming of the Holy Spirit until the Assumption and Coronation of the Virgin Mother of God in Heaven.

V. APPENDIX

A. Approbations
B. Authors and Publishers
C. Current Canonical Explanation

INTRODUCTION

In the first chapter of CITY OF GOD Ven. Mary of Agreda tells about the heavenly enlightenments leading her to begin writing this narrative of the Virgin Mother of God. Only a few sentences are quoted here.

". . . the effect of greater favors and benefits must be a greater fear, reverence, attention and humility."

Words of Divinity: "I desire to make known to mortals how much intercession of Her is worth, who brought restoration of life by giving mortal existence to the immortal God."

"And if men would now seek to please Me by reverencing, believing, and studying the wonders, which are intimately connected with this Mother of Piety, and if they would all begin to solicit her intercession from their whole heart, the world would find some relief."

Can this be true for us today?

THE CONCEPTION

The Sacramental Mysteries wrought by the Most High in the Queen of Heaven from the time of her Immaculate Conception until the Incarnation of the Word in her virginal womb, and how much merit she herself acquired through divine grace by profiting from the favors conferred upon her during those first fifteen years of her life.

THE CONCEPTION

CONTENTS

Chapter 1

GOD'S ETERNAL CREATION

In the beginning was the Word, and the Word
was with God; and the Word was God. He
was in the beginning with God. All things
were made through him, and without him was
made nothing that has been made. In him was
life, and the life was the light of men. . . . It
was the true light that enlightens every man
(and woman) who comes into the world (John
1:1-4,9).

As Creator, God could foresee what would happen to
the human race. God the Son would be the Redeemer,
and the creature to be his Mother would necessarily be
unsurpassable in all purity, knowledge, wisdom and beauty.
Mary would be God's exquisite treasure chest, filled with
the highest mystical graces. In her there would be no taint
of sin, nor any deviation from the will of God, that God
whom she would serve with perfection and the most profound humility.

This woman of mystery is found in the beginning of
the twelfth chapter of Revelation:

And a great sign appeared in heaven: a woman
clothed with the sun, and the moon was under
her feet, and upon her head a crown of twelve
stars (Rev. 12:1).

1

Heaven was made for angels, men and women. But the angels, as most beautiful and perfect creatures, were created in heaven and in the state of grace, making them the first to have the opportunity of meriting the reward of glory. We know that some of them rebelled against the will of God, meriting the eternal punishments which they now suffer.

And there was a battle in heaven; Michael and his angels battled with the dragon, and the dragon fought and his angels (Rev. 12:7).

The angels were shown the glory which could be theirs if they would obey, and also the place of eternal torments if they did not. Lucifer was too proud and filled with self-love. He refused to acknowledge the superiority of a divine person who would make himself so much like a member of the human race. And also he could not accept the fact that a perfect woman could be more powerful than he. He admired himself in his original beauty and grace, and developed a deep hatred toward God and the future human creatures who would be occupying the lost places in heaven.

Lucifer wanted for himself the adoration due to God, and made himself the leader of the other bad angels, who with him, were hurled into the infernal caverns, through the justice and power of God. Instead of Lucifer, he would become known as dragon, serpent, devil and Satan. The arms used by Michael and the other good angels were understanding, reason and truth.

Satan, in all his fury, humiliated himself enough to ask God for permission to tempt the Man-God and the Woman who was to be the Mother of the Redeemer. The Most High answered him, "I give you permission to tempt Christ, so that He may be an example and a teacher in this to all the rest of men. I also give you permission to persecute the Woman, but you must not touch her in regard to the life of her body. It is my will, that Christ and his Mother be not exempt from temptation, and that they be tempted by you like the rest of men."

The way in which the Blessed Virgin conquered Satan in his temptations will be revealed in later chapters.

In the continued reading of the twelfth chapter in the Book of Revelation, one can find a mystical writing about the Woman and the dragon. Ven. Mary of Agreda has written a good explanation of it, which is not included in this abridgment.

> And being with child, she cried out in her travail and was in the anguish of delivery. And another sign was seen in heaven, and behold, a great red dragon having seven heads and ten horns, and upon his heads seven diadems. And his tail was dragging along the third part of the stars of heaven, and it dashed them to the earth; and the dragon stood before the woman who was about to bring forth, that when she had brought forth he might devour her son. And she brought forth a male child, who is to rule all nations with a rod of iron; and her child was caught up to God and to his throne. And the woman fled into the wilderness, where she has a place prepared by God, that there they may nourish her a thousand two hundred and sixty days (Rev. 12:2-6).

God created the first two persons of our human race for his own delight in teaching them how to know, love and serve him. Ven. Mary writes these words about Adam and Eve: "On the sixth day He formed and created Adam, as it were of the age of thirty-three years. This was the age in which Christ was to suffer death, and Adam in regard to his body was so like unto Christ, that scarcely any difference existed. Also according to the soul Adam was similar to Christ. From Adam God formed Eve so similar to the Blessed Virgin, that she was like unto her in personal appearance and figure. God looked upon these two images of the great Originals with the highest pleasure and benevolence, and on account of the Originals He heaped many blessings upon them, as if He wanted to entertain Himself with them and their descendants until the time should arrive for forming Christ and Mary."

Satan was enraged when he saw the happiness of Adam and Eve. He could not rest until his temptations to Eve resulted in her downfall. Adam joined her in sinning against the God of goodness, mercy, justice and love.

As time went on in the propagation of our race, God chose a certain people, the Hebrews, as his own. He sent prophets like Isaiah and Jeremiah, promising the coming of a Messiah who would be their Savior, one who would suffer and die in order to save the souls of mankind and lead them to the glories of heaven. The Hebrew people, under the guidance of Moses, learned about the one true God whom we worship today. Unfortunately, not all remained faithful. How very blessed were those who did. This would be the heritage of the holy maiden of Nazareth.

Chapter 2

MARY ENTERS
SALVATION HISTORY

God's promise to send a Messiah was remembered in prayer by his chosen people for many years. Two of these holy ones were Joachim and Anne, prepared and created by God in a special way, according to his own heart.

Anne was a beautiful maiden, chaste, holy and pure, experienced in exalted contemplation; also very diligent and industrious. She prayed that she would be favored with a holy husband who would share her values and desires. Anne's home was in Bethlehem.

Joachim lived in Nazareth, a town of Galilee, the home of his family and relatives. He was blessed with holy desires, grave and honest, being humble and sincere in all his ways, and he possessed a profound knowledge of the Sacred Scriptures and the prophets.

By the grace of God, Joachim and Anne were united in holy matrimony. Among other virtues, they practiced generosity toward others. Each year they divided the income from their estates into three parts: one part for the Temple in Jerusalem, one to be distributed to the poor, and the remainder for their own necessities.

However, they had one great sorrow. God had not blessed them with a child during all those twenty years of being together. To the Jewish people of those days, being childless was considered a disgrace, and they were met with reproach and insults from some of their neighbors and acquaintances.

In answer to their fervent prayers, the archangel Gabriel was sent by God to tell them they would become the parents of a marvelous daughter. By a divine decree, this daughter would be called MARY, and in her God would find supreme delight. The archangel appeared to Anne in visible form, but to Joachim, in sleep. Anne was told that her daughter would become the Mother of God, the Messiah. This was a secret which she never made known to the child Mary or to Joachim.

Both Joachim and Anne, in their separate prayers, had made a vow that if a child were given to them, it would be consecrated to the service of God in the Temple at Jerusalem. This would be done when the beautiful, sweet little Mary was three years old. Of course, this would be a great sacrifice for her parents, who had loved her so much, to be without her delightful company any longer. God must have consoled their empty hearts in his own blessed ways.

As the time approached for the creation of Mary, God gave new enlightenments to the angel choirs in heaven. Many were chosen to be special attendants to the immaculate virgin who would become the Mother of the Incarnate Word.

From each of the nine choirs of angels one hundred were selected, nine hundred in all, to be her special guardians. Twelve others were appointed to assist Mary in corporeal and visible forms. Eighteen more were given the privilege of exchanging messages from the Queen to his Majesty, and those from the Lord to her. Seventy seraphim, from those closest to the Divinity, were appointed for special enlightenments and consolations to this Princess of Heaven. Among these thousand celestial spirits, Michael and Gabriel are the ones most familiar to us.

In the creation of Mary, God poured forth from the foundation of his wisdom and goodness, the greatest graces and virtues ever to be given to any creature for all eternity. At the very moment of her conception, Mary received these gifts of love in such an overpowering measure as no other saint, nor all of them together, can ever reach.

The first virtues exercised by the tiny little creature in her mother's womb were the three theological virtues, faith, hope and charity, relating immediately to God. Mary recognized the Divinity with all its perfections and its infinite attributes, and the Trinity with its distinction of Persons. She saw in God the object of her happiness and ultimate end, conceiving such an intense appreciation of the Divinity, that not all the seraphim could ever reach such a high degree of fervor and virtue.

From the first moment of her existence, she was wiser, more prudent, more enlightened, and more capable of comprehending God than any other woman would ever be. Quoting from Fiscar Marison's work: "She perceived God as He is and as the Creator and Glorifier; in heroic acts she reverenced Him, praised Him, gave Him thanks for having created her, loved Him, feared Him and adored Him. . . . She recognized the gifts which she had received, although some of them were yet hidden to her, and she gave thanks with profound humility and prostrated herself in the womb of her mother, though yet in a body so small; and by these acts, she merited more than all the saints in the highest state of perfection and sanctity."

God gave Mary knowledge of all his creation: all men and women; all angels in their hierarchies, dignities and operations; the first state of Adam and Eve in their innocence; their deception, guilt, and fall; the resulting misery for the whole human race; the divine resolve to repair it; the nature of the heavens, the stars and planets; purgatory and hell; all plants and animals on the earth; and the beauty of the ocean floor with its water creatures. In Mary, God could satisfy his love and desire to share the beauties of creation with someone who would truly appreciate his infinite goodness and glory.

At this point in the CITY OF GOD writing, Mary of Agreda devotes three more chapters to an explanation of how the twenty-first chapter of the Book of Revelation is applied to Our Lady.

> And I saw a new heaven and a new earth. For the first heaven and the first earth were gone, and the sea was now no more. And I John saw the holy city, the new Jerusalem, coming down out of heaven, from God, prepared as a bride adorned for her husband (Rev. 21:1,2).

Mary, with her innocence and immaculate purity is the new heaven and the new earth. In her, God began to dwell in a new way, different from the way He dwelt in any other creatures. One paragraph of this part of the mystic's writing is quoted:

"On account of the wonderful works, which God had accomplished in the city of Jerusalem, it was a most excellent symbol of her, who was his Mother, the center and the focus of all wonders of the Almighty. For a similar reason it is also a figure of the works of the Church militant and triumphant; both were revealed to the eagle vision of Saint John and he was shown the correspondence and similarity which those two mystical Jerusalems presented. But in an especial manner he viewed as from a watchtower the exalted Jerusalem of the most holy Mary, in which are portrayed and reproduced all the graces, wonders, gifts and excellences of the Church militant and triumphant. Whatever was transacted in Jerusalem, the city of Palestine, and all that it signified together with its inhabitants, is reproduced in the most pure Mary, the holy City of God, and with a greater and more marvelous excellence than in all the rest of heaven and earth and their inhabitants. Hence she is called the new Jerusalem, since all her gifts, her greatness and virtues are new and are the cause of new wonder to the saints. New also, because she came after all the ancient Fathers, Patriarchs and Prophets, and in her were renewed and accomplished all their clamors, their prophecies and promises; new, because she came without the contagion of guilt and under a new dispensation far from the law of sin; new, because she entered into the world triumphant over sin, the devil and the first deceit, thus being the greatest new event since its beginning."

The second chapter explaining the meaning of St. John's writing in the Book of Revelation begins with verse 9:

> And there came one of the seven angels, who had the vials full of the seven last plagues, and spoke with me, saying: "Come, and I will show you the bride, the wife of the Lamb" (Rev. 21:9).

Mary is the immaculate bride of the Lamb, "gold like the purest glass," because she is most pure and like unto the Divinity. The third chapter of this part of writing begins with verse 19:

> And the foundations and the wall were adorned by all manner of precious stones. The first foundation was jasper; the second, sapphire; the third, chalcedony; the fourth, an emerald; the fifth, sardony; the sixth, sardius; the seventh, chrysolite; the eighth, beryl; the ninth, topaz; the tenth, chrysoprase; the eleventh, hyacinth; the twelfth, amethyst (Rev. 21:19,20).

Ven. Mary's writing explains in detail how the jewels represent the virtues of our Queen. Only a few parts are quoted:

Jasper — ". . . variegated tints and durability indicate the constancy and fortitude, which from the moment of her conception was infused into this great Lady in order that during the course of her life she might continue to exercise all the virtues with invincible magnanimity and constancy."

Sapphire — ". . . the Almighty endowed her with the power of communicating tranquility and peace of spirit to those who will ask for her intercession."

Chalcedony — "This foundation-stone signifies that the Most High conceded to her most holy name the power to disperse the clouds of infidelity spread over the earth, and to destroy the errors of heresy, of paganism, idolatry and all uncertainty in matters of the Catholic faith."

Emerald — ". . . the Most High granted her the privilege of insuring a like stability to her devout followers, obtaining for them perseverance and fidelity in the friendship of God and in the practice of virtue."

Sardonyx — ". . . the great Queen of heaven enjoys the power of interceding and obtaining for her clients the efficacious application of the superabundant merits of the Incarnation and Redemption, including also a special devotion toward the mysteries and the life of Christ our Lord through his merits."

Sardius — "This includes her privilege of distributing the influence, the love and the gifts of the Holy Spirit to those who ask in her name."

Chrysolite — "She cooperated by her most burning love toward the salvation of the whole human race."

Beryl — ". . . was conferred upon her the power to endow her servants with fortitude and patience in the tribulations and difficulties of their undertakings."

Topaz — ". . . She knew that the Lord had made her the Teacher and Guide of all the virgins and lovers of chastity, and that through her intercession, she could obtain these virtues and perseverance in them for all her devotees."

Chrysoprase — ". . . signified the most firm hope planted in the heart of the most holy Mary at her conception, and the love with which it was impregnated and embellished . . . that she might obtain the same firmness of hope for her clients."

Hyacinth — ". . . this love of the great Queen for the Redemption from that first instant, earned her the power of demanding that no sinner, how great and abominable soever he might be, should be excluded from the fruit of the Redemption and justification, nor fail to attain eternal life if he invoked the intercession of this powerful Lady and Advocate."

Amethyst — "For her holy name is so powerful that at the mere intimation of it, they (the devils) are overcome and deprived of strength."

In her first vision of the Divinity, Mary was entirely entranced, and the burning love of God in her soul was never interrupted. The visions granted to Mary were far superior to those experienced by the other privileged saints in their life journeys. During the months before her birth, being in full possession of her intellectual faculties, Mary prayed for the human race in heroic acts of adoration, in reverence and love of God, all in the company of her protective angels. As the days came nearer to the time of her birth, she prayed for the Divinity's care and solicitude to keep her safe in every way when she would be entering this world and would have a new existence among the people with whom she would be living.

During all these centuries, Satan was searching through all the world for the woman who would be his enemy, the one who would crush his head with her heel. He was so arrogant that he believed he could destroy her. God concealed many things from Satan, and all through the thirty-three years of Christ's dwelling in our world, Satan was never sure of the identity of our Redeemer until He died on Calvary.

The demon saw that St. Anne was a very virtuous, holy woman. He tried in many ways to give her doubts about her holy pregnancy, but an unknown force prevented him to come closer to her. Failing in his own deceitful tactics, he used the help of two women to be all sorts of annoyance to her. However, St. Anne, in her meek and patient way, was so kind and prayerful, that the women were converted and loved her. God would let no evil come to Mary, his precious treasure, or to Anne, her holy sanctuary.

The birth of Mary happened on September 8, exactly nine months after her immaculate conception. An interior voice of the Lord told Anne that the hour had come, and she prayed for a happy deliverance. The child Mary was ravished into a high ecstasy, coming forth pure and stainless, beautiful and full of grace. With God's love and grace, the birth could be called miraculous. She was clothed like other infants, and treated in all ways as others would be, although she was superior to all mortals and even angels in wisdom. Anne, being free from the toils and labors of other mothers in giving birth, wrapped her in swaddling clothes, and offered this treasure to his Majesty in heaven, saying, "Give me, O my Lord and King, the necessary enlightenment to know your will and to execute it according to your pleasure in the service of my daughter."

With the inspirations of grace, Anne treated Mary as other mothers would do, embracing and caressing her, but with an interior reverence. In showing their veneration to the glorious child, angels sang heavenly music, some of which was audible also to Anne. The greatest wonder was that the Most High sent angels to bring the Mother of the eternal Word, body and soul, into the empyrean heaven. Mary prostrated herself before the Divine Majesty. This was the first time in which the soul of Mary saw the blessed Trinity in unveiled beatific vision. A voice was heard from the throne speaking in the person of the Father: "Our chosen One shall be called MARY, and this name is to be powerful and magnificent. Those that shall invoke it with devout affection shall receive most abundant graces; those that shall honor it and pronounce it with reverence shall be consoled and vivified, and will find in it the remedy of their evils, the treasures for their enrichment, the light which shall guide them to heaven. It shall be terrible against the power of hell, it shall crush the head of the serpent and it shall win glorious victories over the princes of hell." Mary was carried back to St. Anne, who was wrapped in an ecstasy of highest contemplation. (An angel had assumed an aerial body to take the place of the infant while she was before the heavenly throne.)

On the eighth day after the birth, through the aid of angels, Anne was told that the child was to be named Mary, the name chosen for her in heaven. According to the laws at that time, a woman who had given birth to a daughter would be considered impure for two weeks, and should remain in the state of purification for sixty-six days after the birth. When the time had been completed, St. Anne carried her infant daughter to the Temple. St. Anne offered to the priest Simeon the lamb and the turtledove and the rest of the gifts as required. Shedding a few tears of humility, she requested that the priest pray for her and her child.

Satan observed all these happenings, seeing that the mother accomplished all that was written in the law — even begging prayers as a sinner. God had concealed many things from the demon, so he thought they were an ordinary mother and child, even though they might be more perfect and holy than other persons.

Mary was most perfect as an infant. Her nourishment

was like that of others, but less in quantity. She always had a pleasant countenance and never cried for mere annoyance. She was gracious and lovable, and even as a child, she maintained a certain majesty, never showing any childishness. Her father Joachim loved her as a father and a saint, and the infant Mary showed a special love toward him, permitting more tender caresses from him and her gentle and solicitous mother than from others.

When sleeping she enjoyed a special privilege; her interior acts of love, and all other exercises of her faculties which were not dependent on the exterior senses, continued without interruption. Mary did weep and sigh (as far as her age and her dignity of Queen and Mistress would permit) for the sins of the world and for its redemption through the coming of the Savior. Very often she was engaged in the contemplation of divine mysteries and enjoyed the visions and the conversation of his Majesty. Her intercourse with the angels was also very frequent.

Chapter 3

AN ANGEL GUARD FOR GOD'S MASTERPIECE

In her next chapter of revelations Ven. Mary writes more about the angels appointed for the special service of Our Lady. A few paragraphs are quoted.

"The nine hundred angels, which were chosen from the nine choirs, one hundred from each, were selected from the number of those, who had distinguished themselves by their esteem, love and reverence for the most holy Mary. They were made visible to the blessed Virgin under the form of young men in their early years, but of the most exquisite beauty and courteousness. Their bodily forms showed but little resemblance to earthly matter, for they were transparently pure and like animated crystals bathed in glory, similar to a glorified and transfigured body. With their beauty they combined a grave and amiable composure. Their garments covered them in flowing folds, but were resplendent, like the most clear burnished gold, enameled or stained with exquisite shades of color, presenting a most wonderful and varied beauty to the sight. At the same time all this ornament and visible presence seemed of such a kind, that it could not be subject to the sense of feeling nor be touched by the hand, although it could be seen and perceived like the rays of the sun entering into the open window and revealing the atoms of dust in the air. But the splendor of the angels was incomparably more beautiful and pleasing than any light of the sun."

"In addition, all these angels were crowned with wreaths woven of the most tender and exquisite flowers, that sent forth the sweetest fragrance, not of this earth but altogether spiritual and heavenly. In their hands they held palms of wonderful beauty and variety, which were to signify the virtues, which most holy Mary was to exercise, and the victories, which she was to gain by her sanctity and glory."

"The seventy seraphim, who assisted the Queen were of the number of those nearest to the throne of God, who had most signally distinguished themselves in their devotion and admiration toward the hypostatic union of the divine and human nature in the person of the divine Word."

"Whenever these seventy seraphim showed themselves to her in a visible manner, the Queen saw them in the same form in which Isaiah saw them in imagination, that is with six wings. With two they covered the head, wishing to signify by this humble gesture the insufficiency of their intellect for the comprehension of the sacramental mystery at which they were assisting. . . . With the other wings they covered the feet, which are the inferior extremities in closest contact with the earth, referring thereby to the Queen and Mistress of heaven and earth as being human and earthly in nature and acknowledging her as the creature excelling all others in dignity and grandeur above all understanding and calculation of the created mind; moreover they thereby wished to show, that though exalted as seraphim, they could not keep pace with the dignity and excellence of Mary."

"With the wings of their breast they beat the air or seemed to fly, thereby intimating two things: on the one hand, by their incessant motion and flight, the love, the praise and reverence, which they gave to God; on the other, in disclosing their breasts, they wished to serve as it were to the most holy Mary as a most pure mirror of the Divinity."

"The twelve angels are the guardian angels of the twelve gates, of which St. John speaks in the twenty-first chapter of the Book of Revelation (Rev. 21:12). Her Majesty, the Queen, makes use especially of these twelve angels to assist, enlighten and defend her clients in their necessities and particularly in order to draw them from sin, whenever they invoke them and the most holy Mary. These twelve angels appeared in the same corporeal shape as those which I have first mentioned except that they bore palms and crowns, reserved for the devout servants of the Mistress. Their service consisted especially in bringing to her mind the ineffable kindness of the Lord toward the human race, and in inciting her to praise Him and petition Him for the fulfillment of his mercy."

"The eighteen angels, which completed the number of a thousand were those who signalized themselves in their compassion for the sufferings of the incarnate Word. Their reward for this compassion was great. They appeared to most holy Mary in wonderful beauty, bearing many emblems of the Passion and of other mysteries of the Redemption."

"In describing the forms and the ornaments of these angels I have at the same time mentioned some of their perfections and operations, although necessarily in a limited way, if compared to the reality. For they are invisible rays of the Divinity, most alert in their movements and operations, most powerful in strength, most penetrating in their understanding, incapable of mistake, unchangeable in their condition and in their purpose, never forgetting or losing sight of that which once they have undertaken. They are full of grace and glory without any fear of ever losing them. As they are without a body and invisible, therefore whenever God wishes to grant to man the favor of being able to see them, they assume an aerial and apparent body, one that is adapted to the senses and to the object intended."

Chapter 4

A CONSECRATED LIFE

The infant Mary, beginning with her conception, had knowledge and abilities beyond the powers of other children in their first years of life. However, she prudently chose to not show this in her behavior. Therefore, she was silent until she reached the age when other children usually begin to speak. There was an exception, however, in regard to her conversations with the angels and in vocal prayer to God. St. Anne never heard her, and did not know of her daughter's ability to speak during that first year and a half of her infancy.

At times when her mother freed her arms and hands, the little child would grasp the hands of her parents and kiss them with submission and reverent humility. Mary also tried to make them understand that she wished for their blessing, seeming to speak more by her heart's affection than by spoken words. The thoughts of Joachim and Anne were made known to Mary and she never caused them any annoyance. She was perfect in all her actions.

God continued the graces of divine revelations and visions. If at any time one kind of vision or enlightenment was suspended, Mary was enraptured by others. She was taken by the angels to the empyrean heaven many times where she enjoyed the presence of the Divinity. No other person could ever be capable of such favors, and even the mortal nature of Mary would have been deprived of life if she had not been preserved in a miraculous way.

Mary then prayed that she would never offend God in

her speech, wishing to remain silent all her life rather than give any offense to the Author of all beauty and goodness. At the age of eighteen months, Mary spoke her first words to her parents, asking their blessing and acknowledging that from them after God she had her life and being. Anne and Joachim were delighted to see that Mary was also able to walk by herself. Anne embraced her and said, "My daughter and beloved of my heart, blessed and glorious to the Lord be the hour, in which we hear your words and in which you begin to walk in his holy service. Let your words be few, well measured and considered, and let your footsteps be directed aright toward the service and honor of our Creator."

Mary asked that her mother clothe her not in showy garments, but in coarse and poor material of an ash-grey color. Anne answered, "My daughter, I will conform to your desire in regard to the form and color of your dress; but your strength will not permit the coarseness which you desire, and in this regard, I wish that you obey me." Of course, Mary knew the value of obedience and accepted what was provided for her in all humility.

Whenever possible, the holy child gave alms to the poor, and always accompanied the gifts with a prayer for their spiritual good. With humility and obedience, Mary permitted herself to be taught to read and to do other things as other children in that time of life, though she had been given infused knowledge of all things created.

During the remaining year and a half before going to the Temple, Mary and her mother had many conversations about the glories and goodness of God. Anne did not ever reveal the secret of her heart that her daughter was chosen to be the Mother of the Messiah. Joachim and Anne were given the knowledge that it was the will of God for them to bring Mary to the Temple at Jerusalem on the day when she would be three years old. Mary knew the grief that would be in the hearts of her parents to no longer have her with them. She tried to give consolation to her loving mother, saying that when she would be dedicated to God in the Temple, she would be more her daughter than in their own home.

In the revelations written by Ven. Mary of Jesus, the Blessed Virgin Mary is compared to the ancient Ark of the Covenant. That ark was made of incorruptible cedar covered with purest gold. Mary is our mystical ark free from the corruption of actual sin and disorderly passions. Her virtues are the shining gold adornments. In the ark brought to Jerusalem by Solomon, the stone tablets of the law, the vase of manna and the miraculous staff were preserved. In Mary the treasures of Divinity were preserved; she was the beautiful sanctuary of the Word. Among the other titles given in her Litany, we find that she is called "Ark of the Covenant". The sacred Temple in Jerusalem was the proper place for both in the continuing plan of the Most Holy Trinity.

On the appointed day Joachim and Anne, with their beautiful little daughter, made the journey from Nazareth to Jerusalem. They were accompanied by a few of their relatives. Angels again were with them singing songs of praise to God. Their heavenly music was heard only by Mary as she saw again their visible beauty. Her parents were blessed in their hearts with great joy and consolation of spirit. These chosen three offered a devout and fervent prayer to the Lord; Anne and Joachim offering their child to God, and Mary in humility and adoration, offering up herself. She heard a voice from heaven saying, "Come, my Beloved, my Spouse, come to my Temple where I wish to hear your voice of praise and worship."

Her parents brought Mary to the priest, and together they went to the portion of the Temple buildings, where many young girls were brought up in retirement and virtuous habits, until old enough for the state of matrimony. It was a place selected for the first-born daughters of the royal tribe of Juda and the sacerdotal tribe of Levi. At the entrance to these apartments there were fifteen stairs. Other priests came down the stairs to welcome the blessed child. Mary knelt before Joachim and Anne, asking their blessing which they gave her with tenderest tears. Mary hastened upward in fervor and joy, neither turning back nor shedding tears. The priests received her among the other maidens, and Simeon consigned her to the teachers, one of whom was the prophetess Anne. When brought to her teacher, Mary knelt and asked for her blessing and admission to her direction, obedience and counsel. The prophetess Anne received her with pleasure and said, "My daughter, you will find in me a helpful mother and I will take care of you and of your education with all possible solicitude." Mary greeted and embraced the other maidens who were there, offering herself to be their servant, and asking for their instructions concerning the duties of their position, which she would now assume.

Her parents, Joachim and Anne, naturally were sorrowful as they journeyed back to Nazareth, but the Lord, being very pleased with them, gave abundant consolations to their hearts. God cannot be less generous than his creatures.

The child Mary was assigned a place among the rest of the maidens, each of whom occupied a little room. She prostrated herself on the floor, remembered it was holy ground and kissed it. Mary asked the angels to remain with her, reminding her of all she should do; instructing and guiding her so that she would fulfill the will of God with the utmost perfection. Immediately she was transported to heaven, and with new operations of divine light, she saw face to face the Divinity itself. The Person of the Father spoke these words: "My Dove, my beloved One, I desire you to see the treasures of my immutable being and of my infinite perfections, and also to perceive the hidden gifts destined for the souls, whom I have chosen as heirs of my glory and who are rescued by the life-blood of the Lamb. Behold, my daughter, how liberal I am toward my creatures, that know and love Me; how true in my words, how faithful in my promises, how powerful and admirable in my works. Take notice, my Spouse, how ineffably true it is, that he who follows Me does not walk in darkness. I desire that you, as my chosen One, be an eye-witness of the treasures which I hold in reserve for raising up the humble, enriching the poor, exalting the downtrodden, and for rewarding all that the mortals shall do and suffer for my name." Mary asked that she be allowed to make four vows in his presence: the vows of chastity, poverty, obedience and perpetual enclosure in the Temple. The Most High accepted her vows of chastity and poverty, and told her to observe whatever pertains to the other vows. He also spoke these words: "Your desire shall be fulfilled through many other virgins in the coming law of grace; for, to imitate you and to serve Me, they will make these same vows and live together in community and you shall be the Mother of many daughters."

Then Mary enjoyed another vision in a lower state of ecstasy. A part the next paragraph is quoted:

"In this secondary and imaginary vision some of the seraphim closest to the Lord approached her and by his command adorned and clothed her in the following manner. First all her senses were illumined with an effulgent light, which filled them with grace and beauty. Then they robed her in a mantle or tunic of most exquisite splendor, and girded her with a cincture of varicolored and transparent stones, of flashing brilliancy, which adorned her beyond human comprehension. They signified the immaculate purity and the various heroic virtues of her soul. They placed on her also a necklace or collar of inestimable and entrancing beauty, which contained three large stones, symbolic of the three great virtues of faith, hope and charity; this they hung around her neck letting it fall to her breast as if indicating the seat of these precious virtues. They also adorned her hands with seven rings of rare beauty whereby the Holy Spirit wished to proclaim that He had enriched her with his holy gifts in a most eminent degree. In addition to all this the most holy Trinity crowned her head with an imperial diadem, made of inestimable material and set with most precious stones, constituting her thereby as his Spouse and as the Empress of Heaven." Then the Divine voice was heard: "You shall be our Spouse, our beloved and chosen one among all creatures for all eternity; the angels shall serve you and all the nations and generations shall call you blessed."

With heavenly music the holy child was brought back to her place in the Temple. Mary then went to her instructress and gave her all that her mother had left for her comfort and sustenance, with the exception of a few books and clothes. The discreet matron accepted the articles and resolved to take care of Mary in a special way as one destitute and poor; for each of the other maidens possessed her own spending money and a certain sum assigned and destined for wearing apparel and for other necessities according to her inclinations.

The Blessed Virgin Mary gave counsels for perfection in living the vows as women religious profess today.

Obedience
"The vow of obedience is the principal one in religion; for it implies a total renunciation and denial of one's will. By it the religious renounces all jurisdiction or right to say for herself: I will or I will not, I shall or I shall not act; all this she throws aside and renounces by obedience, delivering herself into the hands of her superior. In order to fulfill this obligation it is necessary for you not to be wise in your own conceit, not to imagine yourself still

mistress of your likings, your desires, or your opinion; for true obedience must be of the quality of faith, so that the commands of the superior are esteemed, reverenced and put into execution, without any pretense of examination or criticism."

Poverty

"The vow of poverty is a generous renunciation and detachment from the heavy burden of temporal things. It is an alleviation of the spirit, it is a relief afforded to human infirmity, the liberty of a noble heart to strive after eternal and spiritual blessings."

"The temporal goods are created by the Most High for the sole purpose of sustaining life; having attained this end, the need of them ceases. And as this need is limited, soon and easily satisfied, there is no reason that the care for the immortal soul should be only fitful and temporary, while the hunger after riches should be so perpetual and unintermitting, as it has come to be among men."

"I require of you such a freedom of spirit, as not to attach yourself to anything, be it great or small, superfluous or necessary."

Chastity

". . . it is the virtue of chastity which makes a religious most worthy and like to her Spouse. For it is chastity, which makes her spiritual and withdraws her from earthly corruption, elevating her to angelic life and to a certain resemblance of God himself. This virtue beautifies and adorns all the rest, raises the body to a higher existence, enlightens the mind and preserves in the soul a nobility above all that is corruptible."

"The vow of chastity includes purity of body and soul; this is easily lost, and it is difficult, sometimes, according to the manner of losing it, even impossible to repair.

. . . in order to preserve perfectly this vow, it is necessary to make an inviolable pact with your senses, not to use them, except for what is according to the dictates of reason and for the glory of the Creator."

Ven. Mary received many more counsels for perfection in living the religious vows which are not mentioned here.

Chapter 5

MARY'S EXEMPLARY VIRTUES

In Mary were hidden the treasures of grace beyond all that could be known or imagined by her Temple companions. In all this beauty of soul, the virtue of humility guided her every action. Mary listened to the priest who gave her this advice: "My daughter, as a very young child, the Lord has drawn you to his house and holy Temple; be thankful for this favor and seek to profit by it by striving hard to serve Him in truth and with an upright heart. Acquire all the virtues, in order that you may return from this holy place prepared and fortified against the troubles and the dangers of this world. Obey your Mistress Anne and commence early to bear the sweet yoke of virtue, in order that you may find it more easy to bear during the rest of your life."

At her request, the priest gave her a rule of life to direct her in her occupations: "My daughter, you will assist at the exercises of divine praise and song in honor of the Lord with all reverence and devotion, and always pray to the Most High for the necessities of his holy Temple and of his people, and for the coming of the Messiah. At eight o'clock you will retire for sleep and at the beginning of dawn you will arise in order to praise the Lord until the third hour (this hour corresponds to our nine o'clock in the morning). From the third hour until evening you will occupy yourself in some manual works, in order that you may be instructed in all things. At meals, of which you will partake after your exercises, observe befitting moderation. Then you will go to hear the instructions of your teacher; the rest of the day you will engage yourself in the reading of Holy Scriptures, and in all things be humble, affable, and obedient to the commands of your instructress." The young Mary also received permission to perform such lowly tasks as cleaning the rooms and washing the dishes, and serving the other maidens in various ways.

Mary read much in the sacred writings, and by means of her infused science, she had a wonderful understanding of all their mysteries. Her holy angels assisted her when she conversed with them about all these truths, while she showed profound intelligence and great acuteness.

Ven. Mary of Jesus writes these words to describe this holy Virgin in the Temple: "The beauty, grace, elegance and courteousness of our Queen were incomparable; for all the natural graces and gifts, which were hers in a most perfect degree, were re-enforced by the splendor of supernatural or divine grace, and effected a marvelous union of grace and beauty in all her being and activity enthralling all in love and admiration of her." In the Temple, and during all the remainder of her life, Mary practiced the various virtues in perfection, gaining by her merits an ever-increasing beauty of soul. At her conception, God had blessed her with the theological virtues of faith, hope, and charity; the cardinal virtues of prudence, justice, fortitude and temperance; and what can be called the natural virtues which lead us to do unto others what we would like done to ourselves. In Mary these virtues were supplemented by the gifts and fruits of the Holy Spirit and the Beatitudes. All the thoughts and actions of this glorious creature were only what would lead to the greater glory and love of God.

> "And blessed is she who has believed, because the things promised her by the Lord shall be accomplished" (Luke 1:45).

In these words Elizabeth described the greatness of Mary's faith. We find these words written by Mary of Agreda: "The faith of the most holy Mary was an image of the whole creation and an open prodigy of the divine power, for in her the virtue of faith existed in the highest and the most perfect degree possible; in a certain manner and to a great extent, it made up for the want of faith in other persons." We have been given this great virtue so that we may have a certain and secure knowledge of the Divinity with His mysteries and admirable works. What the angels see in heaven we believe in an obscure manner under the veil of faith. It is a gift which we should cherish and never lose.

Because Mary experienced so many elevating visions and never forgot anything she had learned, we may wonder how she practiced the virtue of faith as other mortals do. There were times when the Most High suspended the influx and activity of her infused knowledge and hid Himself from her by taking away all clear evidence of Himself from her mind. In those times Mary's faith preserved her from any fault. When the Archangel brought her the message of the Incarnation, she merited an ineffable reward for the act of faith necessary to believe such a deep mystery. In witnessing the Passion of Jesus and his Resurrection, she depended upon Catholic faith, which then made her its mistress and foundress.

Our Lady practiced hope as a complement to her virtue of faith. Hope is the virtue which, depending on faith, keeps us from despair and its opposite, which is presumption. In her words to our Franciscan mystic she says: "My daughter, as with two indefatigable wings, my spirit raised its flight by means of faith and hope toward the endless and the highest good, until it rested in union with God through intimate and perfect love."

Charity or love is the greatest of all virtues, and it was practiced by the Blessed Virgin Mary in such a perfect way, that it could make up for whatever might be lacking in the hearts and souls of other creatures. These words of God have been heard many times: "Thou shalt love the Lord thy God with thy whole heart, with thy whole soul, with thy whole mind, and with all thy strength; and thou shalt love thy neighbor as thyself." In Mary we learn that God is to be loved for his own sake, to find our true satisfaction in Him. We learn to esteem Him and appreciate his goodness, and find that nothing else in the world, in comparison with his love, can satisfy our longing hearts.

St. Paul tells us:

> Charity is patient, is kind; charity does not envy, is not pretentious, is not puffed up, is not ambitious, is not self-seeking, is not provoked; thinks no evil, does not rejoice over wickedness, but rejoices with the truth; bears with all things, believes all things, hopes all things, endures all things (I Cor. 13:4-7).

How truly Mary has been called Mother of beautiful love and holy hope.

In CITY OF GOD Ven. Mary of Jesus writes many words about the virtue of prudence in general and also its operations in the Queen of Heaven. Prudence can be called the correct use of our understanding in guiding our actions. It can be influenced by our past experiences. Mary was gifted in its excellence; her memory was so exceptional that she never forgot anything she had learned. We invoke her as "Virgin most prudent" when we pray her litany, a prayer of the Catholic Church.

Three kinds of prudence are explained in Ven. Mary's revelations: political prudence, purgative prudence, and that of a soul already purified or perfect. All were Our Lady's in perfection. "Political prudence in general is that which ponders and weighs all that is to be done and reduces it to the dictates of reason, eschewing all that is not just and good. The purgative or purifying prudence is that which disposes and selects all things in such a way as to rectify the heart by divine contemplation toward all celestial things. The prudence of the purified or perfect soul is that which directs and centers all the affections upon the highest Good, as if no other object existed."

The virtue of prudence can be considered under another aspect. Philosophers have mentioned five other points of this virtue, namely: docility, reasonableness, cleverness, circumspection and caution. "Docility is the good judgment and readiness of the creature to be taught by others better informed than itself, and a disposition not inflated by its own insight and wisdom. Reasonableness, or the power of drawing correct inferences, consists in reasoning without error from generally understood principles to the particular course of action in each single case. Cleverness is a diligent attention and practical application of our activity to that which happens, enabling us to judge rightly and follow the best course of action, just as docility is attention to the teachings of others. Circumspection is a just consideration of the circumstances connected with each good work; for it is not sufficient that the end of our actions be good, but it is necessary to consider the opportuneness of the circumstances. Cautiousness is a discreet attention to the dangers or impediments, so that when they occur under cover of virtue or unexpectedly, we may not be found rash or unprepared."

Mary's docility allowed her to be taught by others although she had received the plenitude of knowledge from the moment of her immaculate conception. In reasonableness she pondered in her heart the mysterious events in the life of her Son, reasoning from cause to cause, enabling her to perform a perfect response as the years of her life continued. In cleverness Mary was always alert and skillful in noticing and performing what was necessary and good in her relationships with others. In circumspection, Mary's actions were so accomplished that no point of perfection was missing. Her reasonable and pleasing manners met with success in teaching, admonishing, consoling, beseeching and correcting her neighbor. Cautiousness was also practiced by the virtuous Queen in perfection whenever necessary. In striving for perfection ourselves, we are told to unite the simplicity of the dove with the prudence of the serpent.

The next chapter in our mystic's writing is concerned with the cardinal virtue of justice which urges us to give to each individual what is due in dignity and consideration, remembering what we would like to have done to ourselves.

Legal justice refers to the public and common good. Mary observed it to the letter in the prescriptions of the old Law, when she conformed to the rites of the purification ceremonies, even though being exempt from all sin herself.

After the Ascension of Jesus, Mary assisted the Apostles in the government of the primitive Church. She managed the distribution of the common property for the sustenance and other necessities of each individual. She never handled the money herself, but gave directions on how it should be distributed. Besides her extraordinary knowledge of each soul, she made use of prayer and divine enlightenment, giving direction and counsel in perfect equity and without acceptation of persons. Quoting again: "As regard to particular judgments, no injustice could ever find a place in the most pure heart of most holy Mary; for she could never be imprudent in her suspicions, or rash in her judgments, nor was she troubled by doubts; nor, if she had any, would she ever decide them unkindly for the worse part."

Truthfulness also is a part of justice. Lying, deceitful simulation, hypocrisy, boastfulness, and irony are to be avoided.

Above all, Mary never failed in giving to God all that we creatures owe to our benevolent Creator. We do this in our fervent worship and reverence, with an unfathomable gratitude and a desire to never offend in thought, word, or deed.

To explain the virtue of fortitude and its meaning in Our Lady's life, we begin with a quotation:

"The moderation of the irascible passions by the virtue of fortitude is made up of two elements or kinds of activity: to give way to anger in conformity with reason, propriety and honor, and to repress unreasonable anger and passion, whenever it is more useful to restrain than to allow them to act. For as well the one or the other can be praiseworthy or blamable according to the end in view and the circumstances of the affair in hand. The first of these two kinds of operation of this virtue is properly called fortitude, being called by some teachers pugnacity. The second is called patience, which is the more noble and excellent kind of fortitude, and is possessed and exercised principally by the saints."

In the Blessed Virgin all the passions were well ordered, her reason being subject to God who governed her actions. At times the demon tried to place obstacles in her path, but with the virtue of fortitude, she overcame him. She never showed anger in her relationships with other people. In the practice of patience she was most admirable. "The whole life of the sovereign Queen was a continual suffering and tribulation, especially during the life and passion of our Redeemer, Jesus Christ. Her patience during this time exceeds the comprehension of all creatures; and only the Lord who imposed this suffering upon her, could worthily understand its greatness."

Another part of fortitude is magnanimity, calling us to pursue the doing of great things while also practicing humility, which is truth, referring all the glory to God. Mary did everything in a great and noble way.

The virtue of temperance teaches us to govern ourselves by reason, not by desires. "Therefore a certain decorous honorableness and comeliness distinguish this virtue, by which the reason is enabled to preserve its rule, although the indomitable passions are hardly ever inclined to listen or yield to it willingly."

Abstinence and sobriety are sometimes difficult for us to practice. Mary did feel hunger and thirst, but she never sought after delicacies, nor did she take food merely for pleasure, but only in order to supply her natural wants and needs with nothing superfluous. Mary chose to never eat meat, and never ate more than once a day except when she lived with her husband Joseph, and when she accompanied Christ in his travels. At all times she was wonderful in her temperance.

Our Lady teaches that the gifts of the Holy Spirit, wisdom, understanding, counsel, fortitude, knowledge, piety and fear of the Lord, add beauty to the soul and give strength and joy in doing good. Their limitations lie only on the part of the subject on which they act. In themselves they do not admit of any limitation.

We learn how the gifts act upon the virtues: "The gift of wisdom communicates to the soul a certain kind of taste by which it can distinguish the divine from the human without error, throwing all its influence and weight in all things against those inclinations which arise from human ignorance and folly; this gift is related to charity. The gift of understanding serves to penetrate into the understanding of divine things and gives a knowledge of them overwhelmingly superior to the ignorance and slowness of the natural intellect; while that of knowledge searches the most obscure mysteries and creates perfect teachers to oppose human ignorance; these two gifts are related to faith. The gift of counsel guides, directs and restrains man within the rules of prudence in his inconsiderate activity. It is closely related to this its own virtue. That of fortitude expels disorderly fear and gives strength to human weakness; it is superadded to the cardinal virtue of that name. Piety makes the heart kind, takes away its hardness and softens it against its own impiety and stubbornness; it is related to religion. The fear of God lovingly humiliates the soul in opposition to pride, and is allied to humility."

These gifts can raise the soul to a union with the Divinity in a spiritual bond of eternal peace. "Such a happiness, however, is the lot of a few, and only by experience can it actually be known, who does attain it."

In the Mother of God these gifts of the Holy Spirit were proportionate to her dignity and far beyond whatever can be acquired by all other creatures.

In Chapter XIV of the second part of her first volume, Ven. Mary explains the five kinds of visions enjoyed by the Queen of Heaven. Of ordinary creatures they require a great purification and caution. The Blessed Virgin was different, being pure and immaculate from her very beginning.

The visions explained are called (1) a clear vision of the Divinity, (2) abstractive visions, (3) intellectual visions and revelations, (4) imaginary visions, and (5) corporeal visions.

In this abridgment they are not explained, and the ending words of this chapter are quoted: "I submit myself in these things to the doctors and teachers of the spiritual life."

Chapter 6

GOD'S PLAN FOR MARY BEGINS TO UNFOLD

We now return to the sweet little Mary in the Temple, where she was filled with more of God's wonders and favors of his love as the days went by. Mary's joy-filled soul gave such a return of love and praise to her Creator, that she was elevated to a higher dignity and blessedness than even the angels can experience in their worship and service to God.

Though a child in years, she was like an adult in her wisdom and knowledge. Mary understood the Scriptures and spent much time in reading them, especially the prophets Isaiah and Jeremiah, and the Psalms. Many times her fervent prayers were requesting the coming of the Redeemer. She often inquired about these mysteries of the Messiah in her conversations with the angels, thus extending her own knowledge of divine teachings. She knew that the Holy One would become an infant, be born of a virgin mother, suffer and die as all men are destined to do.

With all the abundance of grace, Mary was to learn that suffering is a treasure in the eyes of God. The divine words: "It is also conformable to my equity and providence, that the mortals should attain and merit for themselves the crown of glory through hardships and the cross, since my only begotten Son is to merit it by the same means in human flesh." Mary was to dispose herself for tribulations and sorrows in her pure love for God.

She was told that her father Joachim would soon leave this mortal life for the eternal life awaited in limbo. When the hour for his passing arrived, Mary sent her angels, asking God to make them visible to her father for his consolation. This request was answered, and the angels told Joachim that his daughter Mary was the chosen one to be the Mother of the Word Incarnate. Anne, who was at his bedside, also heard these words. At that moment Joachim lost the use of his speech, and his agony began in a struggle between joy at this message and the pain of death. The angels carried his holy soul to the limbo of the patriarchs and the just souls awaiting the opening of the gates of heaven. This happened about six months after Mary's entrance into the Temple. We are told that Joachim died at the age of sixty-nine. He was forty-six years of age when he married St. Anne. Mary asked the Lord to console, govern and assist her mother Anne in her solitude after the death of her husband. We can imagine how wonderfully God answered this request.

Our Lady gave this advice to Ven. Mary of Agreda when informing her about the value of suffering: "Rejoice and congratulate yourself in your sufferings, and whenever the Almighty deigns to send you any, hasten to meet it and welcome it as one of his blessings and pledges of his glorious love."

At this time in Mary's young life, the Most High chose to send spiritual afflictions to this greatest of all his lovers. The wonderful visions and caresses ceased. The angels were no longer visible. Mary was to learn by experience the science of suffering. In her dereliction she thought she might not have been sufficiently grateful for the spiritual favors lavished upon her. Her sighs and loving desires were most pleasing to the Lord in ways which He alone understands. It came as a great surprise to our little Queen. She felt entirely forsaken and left alone in the dark night occasioned by the absence of her Beloved. The words of the Scripture Canticle are an expression of her holy desires. Our heavenly Lady suffered more spiritual torments and anxieties than all the saints together in the fear of having lost Him.

Mary's great perfections did not escape the notice of Satan. He was enraged against her. With his deceitful wiles he attempted to make her commit a fault in her virtuous thoughts and actions. But an unknown force would not permit him to harm her. He then called for a council with all his companion fiends, seeking their ideas in a way to make her fall as Eve had been deceived. Satan said, "Her wisdom enrages me, her modesty irritates me, her humility annihilates me and oppresses me, and her whole behavior provokes me to unbearable wrath. I abhor her more than all the children of Adam."

It was resolved that a new attempt should be effected through the other maidens who were her companions. The temptations of the devils succeeded in making the other Temple maidens develop a jealousy and hatred toward the holy child Mary. They accused her of many faults which were not at all true. One day they took her to an empty room and poured out insults and unkind deeds, causing such a commotion that the priests and the instructress came to see what was happening. Mary was silent, and her tormentors accused her of many faults, saying she was not worthy to remain in the Temple. The priests and Anne believed the accusations and took Mary to another room, and there they severely reprehended her. In all of this, Mary most humbly accepted their words and promised to amend her conduct.

She went to her companions and asked their pardon. They received her this time with a bit of good will, thinking her tears were from the punishment and warnings of the priests and the teacher Anne. Again, the attempts of the devils were unsuccessful in doing any spiritual harm to God's favorite daughter, but only made her more beautiful in his sight.

The unkind treatment of the other girls continued and Mary accepted it with her unconquerable humility. However, God intervened and spoke to the priest in his sleep, saying, "My servant Mary is pleasing in my eyes, and she is my perfect and my chosen one; she is entirely innocent of anything of which she is accused." Anne, the instructress of the maidens, received the same revelation. In the morning they met and found that both had received the identical message. They called Mary and asked her pardon, offering her all the reparation necessary, and from that time on they attended to her and observed her with new reverence and affection. God was very pleased with Mary, but He continued to hide himself for ten years, except for a few brief times when He showed himself for the consolation of his Beloved. This was done with less lavishness and tenderness than in the first years of her childhood. These sufferings continued until Mary was twelve years old.

Then on a certain day the angels gave her the message that her holy mother Anne would soon die. God gave Mary a great favor, commanding the angels to carry her to her mother's bedside, while another angel took her place in the Temple. Anne and Mary spoke many holy words together, but again, St. Anne did not reveal the secret that her daughter was to be the Mother of our Redeemer. As Mary held St. Anne in her arms, the soul of the holy matron was received into the glory of eternal life and the dearest of all daughters in the world was carried back to the Temple.

A brief description of St. Anne is found in this book of Ven. Mary's revelations: "She was of medium stature, somewhat smaller than her daughter, most holy Mary; her face was rather round, of a suffused whiteness, her countenance was always equable and composed." Anne was fifty-six years old when she died, twenty-four years old when she married St. Joachim, forty-four years of age when she gave birth to Mary, and forty-eight when St. Joachim died. "Because of her having such a daughter and of her being the grandmother of the Word made man, all the nations may call the most fortunate St. Anne blessed."

In God's own chosen time, after waiting so long, the angels again came to Mary in their visible splendor. They told her that the Lord had commanded them to conceal themselves from her sight during the time when He himself was hidden from her. They said, "If the Beloved did not hide himself, He would not be sought after with that anxiety which is caused by his absence, nor would the soul renew its affections, nor increase in the appreciation due to that Treasure."

An abstractive vision of the Divinity was then given to most holy Mary. Our Queen's affections and anxieties, her patience, her humility, her fortitude and her constancy were rewarded with supreme delight, satisfying all her desires. "Our Princess issued from this vision altogether renovated and made godlike; full of the new science of the Divinity and of the hidden sacraments of the King."

At the age of thirteen and a half years, Mary had another abstractive vision in which her loving God commanded her to enter the state of matrimony. We can imagine the distress which came to her because she had made a vow of chastity and had never wanted to have a husband. Yet, though she felt some sadness, she resigned herself entirely into the hands of the Lord. His Majesty's words were these: "Mary, let not your heart be disturbed, for your resignation is acceptable to Me and my powerful arm is not subject to laws; by my disposition that will happen, which is most proper for you."

In the meantime, the high priest Simeon was told in his sleep that he must make arrangements for the marriage of Mary. He was instructed to tell the other priests that she was left alone and an orphan. It was the custom that the firstborn maidens should not leave the Temple without being provided for, and Mary should then be married to whomever it seemed good to them. According to the law, the husband of Mary had to be of the house and race of David. A day was appointed for all the free and unmarried men of that race, now living in Jerusalem, to come together in the Temple. It was the very day on which Mary completed her fourteenth year. The Lord spoke to Mary, "I will find for you a perfect man conformable to my heart and I will choose him from the number of my servants; my power is infinite, and my protection and aid shall never fail you."

Among the men gathered was Joseph, one of the descendants of the royal race of David. "He was thirty-three years of age, of handsome person and pleasant countenance, but also of incomparable modesty and gravity; above all he was most chaste in thought and conduct, and most saintly in all his inclinations. From his tenth year he had made and kept the vow of chastity. He was related to the Virgin Mary in the third degree, and was known for the utmost purity of his life, holy and irreprehensible in the eyes of God and of men."

By divine intervention, Joseph was the one chosen to take the beautiful and pure Virgin Mary as a spouse. Together they left Jerusalem and went to Nazareth. They were visited by friends and relatives according to the custom of newlyweds at that time.

When left alone, they discovered that each of them had made a vow of chastity. Joseph was filled with respect and reverence for Mary. Between the two spouses there arose a contest about who would serve the other. But Mary, being the most humble of all creatures, insisted that the man is the head of the family and that she should be the servant of Joseph. "On such heavenly beginnings

was founded the home and the married life of the most
holy Mary and saint Joseph."

In the last two chapters of her first volume, Mary of
Agreda describes the virtues of Mary as the ideal wife,
using the figurative language of the final chapter of
Proverbs.

> When one finds a worthy wife,
> > her value is far beyond pearls.
> Her husband, entrusting his heart to her,
> > has an unfailing prize.
> She brings him good, and not evil,
> > all the days of her life.
> She obtains wool and flax
> > and makes cloth with skillful hands.
> Like merchant ships,
> > she secures her provisions from afar.
> She rises while it is still night,
> > and distributes food to her household.
> She picks out a field to purchase;
> > out of her earnings she plants a vineyard.
> She is girt about with strength,
> > and sturdy are her arms.
> She enjoys the success of her dealings;
> > at night her lamp is undimmed.
> She puts her hands to the distaff,
> > and her fingers ply the spindle.
> She reaches out her hands to the poor,
> > and extends her arms to the needy.
> She fears not the snow for her household;
> > all her charges are doubly clothed.
> She makes her own coverlets;
> > fine linen and purple are her clothing.
> Her husband is prominent at the city gates
> > as he sits with the elders of the land.

She makes garments and sells them,
    and stocks the merchants with belts.
She is clothed with strength and dignity,
    and she laughs at the days to come.
She opens her mouth in wisdom;
    and on her tongue is kindly counsel.
She watches the conduct of her household,
    and eats not her food in idleness.
Her children rise up and praise her;
    her husband, too, extols her:
"Many are the women of proven worth,
    but you have excelled them all."
Charm is deceptive and beauty fleeting;
    the woman who fears the Lord is to be praised.
Give her a reward of her labors,
    and let her works praise her at the city gates.

Mary's extraordinary gifts and her heroic use of them made her valiant and precious, with a value far beyond pearls. Being the beautiful fountain of virtue and grace, nothing could be less than perfection in Mary's house-wife duties for Jesus and Joseph. With all these activi-ties, her interior faculties never ceased in their adoration and awareness of the omnipotent God.

The vineyard Mary planted is the holy Church, not only by giving us her holy Son to form it, but by being his coadjutrix, and after his Ascension, by guiding the Apos-tles as Mistress of the Church.

Mary had a great and generous love for the poor. She distributed the inheritance of her parents to the Temple and to those persons most in need of life's necessities. With her own hands she performed many works of mercy.

Although being herself completely innocent of any trans-gressions against the God of mercy, she chastised her vir-ginal body by penances, watchings, fasts, and prostrations in the form of a cross — all for us in our human family.

The "fine linen and purple" as her clothing were the purple of charity, the white of chastity and purity, the azure of hope, and all the other gifts and graces which adorned her in all their variety and beauty. She was and always will be our intercessor at the Divine throne.

THE INCARNATION

The Mysteries of the Life of the Holy Mother of God from the Incarnation of the Divine Word in her virginal womb to the return of the Holy Family from Egypt.

THE INCARNATION

CONTENTS

Chapter 1

PREPARATION FOR BECOMING THE MOTHER OF GOD

After the passing of many ages the time was approaching for the fulfillment of the great mystery of the Incarnation, as planned in the divine decree of the most Holy Trinity. What a source of eternal wonder and awe for all persons in our weakened human race! God becoming man — perhaps the most important reason for the creation of Mary, who leads us all in the virtues of faith and humility. She alone was enlightened beyond our comprehension.

As the faithful wife of St. Joseph, no daily household duties were ever neglected. Mary also met other people who were influenced by her holiness. A spiritual radiance seemed to flow from the Virgin, and persons who came in contact with her felt a desire to lead a more virtuous life. Mary was aware of these graces and prayed that no glory would come to her, but only to God, the Author of all glory.

Six months and seventeen days intervened between Mary's espousal and the Incarnation of the Word. God chose to prepare her for this great event during the nine days preceding the message of the Archangel Gabriel.

On this first of the nine days of preparation, Mary arose from her couch at midnight, and in a prostrate position, began her usual prayers and exercises. Angels spoke to her with these words, "Spouse of our King and Lord, arise for his Majesty calls you." Mary said words similar to these: "Most high and powerful Master, what do you wish to do with me?"

Immediately she was favored with an abstractive vision more exalted and profound than others in the past. Deeper secrets of the Divinity were revealed to Mary. God gave her a thorough knowledge of his creative acts as recorded in the first chapter of the Book of Genesis. She knew the size and formation of our planet earth: its longitude, latitude, depth and caverns, with its countries, climes, and inhabitants. The nature of the angels was also revealed to her, including their conditions, diversity, hierarchies, offices, grades and virtues; also the bad angels and the cause of their fall. God manifested to Mary his holy desires for the redemption of the human race of which she was a member.

The future Queen of Heaven did not fail the Almighty in her correspondence to all these graces. All that day she fulfilled his pleasure in asking for the redemption of mankind, and prayed that the time for the coming of the Messiah would be soon, as promised in the prophecies of the past. With deepest humility she prostrated herself to the ground and prayed in the form of a cross.

At midnight on the second of the nine days of preparation, Mary again arose to begin her time of prayer, awaiting God's call. Again she was favored with an abstractive vision in which she saw the continuing creative power of our God. She saw how the Most High divided the waters and established the firmament with its heavenly bodies. She was inflamed with praise and admiration for the omnipotence of God.

In Mary the two natures, that of the Divine and that of the human, were to be united in her womb so that she truly could be called the Mother of God. She was to receive a proportionate knowledge and dignity, making her inferior only to God, and superior to all that is not God.

Mary learned the perfect order of the cosmos with its heavenly bodies; the qualities, conditions, greatness and movements of the planets and stars. In addition to the knowledge of the elements which influence our weather patterns, she was given sovereignty over them and they would obey her wishes. Mary never used this power for her own convenience in moderating the rigors of the cold and the discomfort of the heat. However, in the journey to Egypt, she commanded these weather conditions to give no discomfort to the Infant Jesus.

Again on this second novena day, Our Lady was to continue her supplications in prayer that the Messiah would make no delays in coming to redeem his people.

God continued to increase the virtues and heavenly loveliness in Mary, his Beloved, through the abstractive visions granted to her. On the third day of preparation for the conception of the Incarnate Word, Mary was given further graces and powers to make her a reflection of the divine attributes. Beyond our comprehension are the treasures of knowledge and love bestowed on her.

Mary learned when and how the waters of the ocean were formed, separating the earth from the sea, how the lakes and rivers came into existence, and the way they flowed back to the oceans. She was shown how God provided for many needs of his creatures in the various plants produced on the earth: herbs, trees, flowers, roots, fruit and seeds — and how they serve for the use of man. Mary, as Mistress of all, used this knowledge at times in her assistance to the poor.

She became more Godlike in her kindness and mercy. She was willing to suffer all trials, sorrows, illnesses, pains and afflictions for the salvation of the other souls brought into existence by a loving Creator. Our Lady would have done anything to make reparation for the ingratitude of so many in our human race. As all other saintly souls, she knew her unbounded gifts were to be shared with others. This vision brought her increasing fervor, and she continued to pray as she had been commanded during the other hours of this third day.

The beginning of the fourth day also found Mary absorbed in the contemplation of God. Again in an abstractive vision more divine favors were granted to her. She received knowledge of how the luminaries of heaven were formed for indicating night and day, the seasons, the days and the years; their material substance, their form, size and movements, the inequality of the planets and the number of the stars.

Divine power and wisdom have no limits except those of the will in the limited creature. Mary's will was in complete conformity with God so that she met all his desires. Her enlightenments included the new law of grace to be established by the Redeemer. She knew the gifts and blessings prepared for men, and the desire of God that all should be saved. In this vision Mary suffered bitter anguish in her loving heart in the knowledge that not all souls were to be saved by the sufferings of the promised Redeemer. For her consolation the Most High spoke these words: "Accept, my Spouse, the gifts which the blind and ignorant world in its unworthiness despises and is incapable of receiving and understanding."

Mary multiplied her prayers and meritorious works to hasten the Incarnation of our holy Redeemer, Jesus Christ.

The fifth day of divine revelations was a continuation of the divine plan to make the immaculate Mary a holy sanctuary for the Incarnate Word. Mary was told that only a small number of souls would be God's chosen ones with a true knowledge and grateful love of Him. Greater would be the number of the ungrateful and reprobate.

The holy Virgin pleaded with God for his mercy to those in danger of losing their souls in everlasting torments. She saw in the Lord all human creatures of the past, present and future, the position of each one in creation, and the final destiny of each.

Another part of this vision gave Mary a thorough knowledge of all the animals living in the waters of the seas and rivers. She knew each variety of fish, large and small. Also made known to her were the animals living on earth in the fields and the woods, with their conditions, peculiarities, and their usefulness for the good of men. She was shown the birds of the air in their many colors, sizes, and differences in their chirpings and songs. Besides knowing the animals, Mary was given the power to command them. She used this power when Jesus was born in Bethlehem, giving the ox and the ass the command to provide warmth for the Divine Infant.

Following this vision, the Blessed Virgin continued her prayers and petitions as she had been inspired by the Most High, pleading again for the coming of the Messiah. She did not know that very soon her prayer would be answered.

The sixth day of illuminations for preparing Mary to be the faultless Mother of God began as usual with her midnight prayers, this time with even more fervor and intensity as she pleaded with all her heart for the coming of the Redeemer.

She was raised in abstractive vision before the Divinity to understand the greatness of God's creation of man. This vision provided more heavenly effects and a deeper insight into the attributes of God. Mary saw how at the command of the Lord the earth brought forth the various living beings in all their kinds and species: some, beasts of burden to assist man; wild beasts, more fierce and untamed; reptiles which remain close to the earth. Our Lady knew their qualities, strengths, and the useful purposes which they serve. God made all these creatures for the benefit of man.

Mary understood the divine decree, "Let us make man to our image and likeness." The Virgin was given a profound knowledge of the parts of the human body: the number of the bones, veins, arteries, nerves and ligatures; the temperaments, nutrition, growth and locomotion; the causes of sickness and their cures; the intimate union of the soul with the body. The perfections of the first man and woman were revealed to her, and also their loss of grace when tempted by the demon.

Mary knew and understood that she too was a daughter of these first parents. She felt profound sorrow for the ingratitude of mankind and strove to render to God the gratitude and obedience which others had neglected or overlooked. Ven. Mary of Agreda writes that this vision continued for nine hours and ended at the third hour of the day.

Every possible divine gift to a creature was bestowed upon the beautiful Virgin Mary in its own degree of perfection. On this seventh day Our Lady arose and was immersed in the glories of Divinity. Angels carried her bodily into the empyrean heaven, while one of them remained in her place of prayer to represent her in a corporeal form. This had happened to her before when she entered the Temple, but now it was more meaningful. A voice from the Most High spoke these words: "Our Spouse and chosen Dove, our gracious Friend, who has been found pleasing in our eyes and has been chosen among thousands: We wish to accept you anew as our Bride, and therefore we wish to adorn and beautify you in a manner worthy of our design." The angels recognized the humble maiden as their sovereign. Mary was to be clothed and adorned with precious jewels to symbolize the graces and privileges of a Queen. Such was to be the immediate preparation for the miracle of the Incarnation.

An exquisite dazzling white tunic or robe was put on her as a symbol of her purity. Over the robe was placed a girdle, as a symbol of the holy fear, which was infused into her. It was decorated with beautiful jewels of extreme refulgence. At this the heavenly Princess understood why the gift of Fear of the Lord should be found in each of his creatures. Most beautiful and abundant hair held together with a brilliant golden clasp was the next adornment. This indicated her privilege of spending her entire life in exalted and divine thoughts, a participation in the wisdom and knowledge of God. Sandals were placed on her feet to indicate that her steps, always aiming for the greater glory of God, would be most beautiful. Bracelets adorned her arms, and rings were placed on her fingers. She was filled with magnanimity for undertaking great works, exalted in purpose. A necklace set with brilliant jewels was added. This indicated a renewal of the virtues of faith, hope and charity as necessities in the Incarnation and Redemption mysteries. Earrings of gold filigreed with silver were the last of the jewelry adornments. These were to prepare her ears for the Archangel Gabriel's message.

In all this beauty and adornment the Virgin Mary stood before the Lord, most beautiful and charming in the utmost perfection and unparalleled sanctity.

During the eighth day of preparation, Mary pleaded with many words and sighs for the salvation of her human brothers and sisters. Her prayers were heard with great pleasure by the God who had promised to send a Savior. The Most High answered in words like these: "Come to Me, and do not be dismayed in the consciousness of your human nature; I am He, that raises the humble, and fills with riches those that are poor."

The angels again raised Mary to the Throne of God, where the celestial spirits gazed with wonder and admiration at the beauty of one woman so blessed by heavenly gifts.

An abstractive vision again enclosed her with favors of light and purification especially reserved for this day. His Majesty assured her that He would grant whatever she asked. Her most honest reply was given with faith, hope and love, "Let the day of your promises dawn upon us, O my God, let your words be fulfilled, and let the Messiah, expected for so many ages, arrive."

All things were transformed within her as she was enveloped with the fiery clouds of the Divinity. With unceasing praise, love and gratitude, Mary was transported back to earth where she spent the remainder of another very special day of her life in glorious humility.

The last day of the novena of preparation had arrived. That night during the hour of greatest silence, Mary was again called by God. Her responding words were these: "My heart is prepared, my Lord and exalted Sovereign; let your divine pleasure be fulfilled in me."

As had been done before, Mary was brought by the angels to the Throne of the Most High, where his Majesty seated her at his side, a place which would be hers forever as Queen of angels and men. The whole of creation, which Mary had been shown only in parts before, now was revealed to her in its entirety. She learned how the divine will governs and preserves the harmony, order, connection and dependence of each of his creatures in its place and mode of existence. These words were spoken to Mary: "You my Spouse, shall be my chosen One and you have found grace in my sight; and therefore I make you Mistress of all these goods and I give you dominion and possession of them all, so that, if you are a faithful spouse according to my wishes, you may distribute and dispose of them according as you desire and according as your intercession shall direct; for this is the purpose, for which they are given into your possession."

An important lesson for us to remember is that with every new grace given to Mary, there was an increase in her profound humility. A crown was placed on the head of Mary by the Blessed Trinity, consecrating her as Queen of all creation. It was fitting that God should first make her Queen before making her Mother of the Prince of eternities.

Chapter 2

INCARNATION OF THE WORD

At the command of God, the time had arrived for the Archangel Gabriel to reveal to Mary that she was chosen to be the Mother of the Messiah. Other angels accompanied him as he descended from the highest heaven to the humble cottage which was the dwelling place of holy Mary.

Ven. Mary of Agreda describes the archangel: "The appearance of the great prince and legate was that of a most handsome youth of rarest beauty; his face emitted resplendent rays of light, his bearing was grave and majestic, his advance measured, his motions composed, his words weighty and powerful, his whole presence displayed a pleasing, kindly gravity and more of godlike qualities than all the other angels until then seen in visible form by the heavenly Mistress."

Our Spanish mystic also describes the young Virgin: "The bodily shape of the heavenly Queen was well proportioned and taller than is usual with other maidens of her age; yet extremely elegant and perfect in all its parts. Her face was rather more oblong than round, gracious and beautiful, without leanness or grossness; its complexion clear, yet of a slightly brownish hue; her forehead spacious yet symmetrical; her eyebrows perfectly arched; her eyes large and serious, of incredible beauty and dovelike sweetness, dark in color with a mixture tending toward green; her nose straight and well shaped; her mouth small with red-colored lips, neither too thin or too thick. All the gifts of nature in Her were perfectly symmetrical and beautiful. . . . Her garments were humble and poor, yet clean, and of a dark silvery hue, somewhat like the color of ashes, and they were arranged and worn without pretense, but with the greatest modesty and propriety."

The Archangel Gabriel came into the presence of the holy Virgin and spoke these words: "Hail full of grace, the Lord is with you, blessed are you among women."

A little disturbance was felt by Mary because of her great humility. The archangel continued, "Do not fear, Mary, for you have found grace before the Lord; behold, you shall conceive a Son in your womb, and you shall give birth to Him, and you shall name Him Jesus; He shall be great, and He shall be called Son of the Most High."

Our Lady replied, "How shall this happen, that I conceive and bear; since I know not, nor can know man?" Gabriel explained that the Holy Spirit would overshadow her by a new presence, so that the Holy of holies could be born of her. Mary was also told that her cousin Elizabeth had conceived a son in her sterile years because nothing is impossible with God.

The holy Virgin remembered the prophecies and divine promises concerning the Redemption of all the human race; all this would depend on her reply of acceptance.

Mary's pure soul was elevated in divine love, in such an intense way that her heart was contracted and three drops of her most pure blood flowed to the natural place for the act of conception. At the same moment, she pronounced the words, "Be it done to me according to your word."

Ven. Mary writes: "At the pronouncing of this 'fiat,' so sweet to the hearing of God and so fortunate for us, in one instant, four things happened. First, the most holy body of Christ our Lord was formed from the three drops of blood furnished by the heart of most holy Mary. Secondly, the most holy soul of the same Lord was created, just as the other souls. Thirdly, the soul and the body united in order to compose his perfect humanity. Fourthly, the Divinity united Itself in the Person of the Word with the humanity, which together became one composite being in hypostatical union; and thus was formed Christ true God and Man, our Lord and Redeemer."

At the moment of conception all creation was set in motion. The stars grew more brilliant, the sun, moon and planets hastened their movements; the birds sang joyous new songs; the plants and the trees became more fruitful and fragrant; other creatures also felt a vivifying change.

For hell it was a cause of new despair. A divine force hurled the demons into their darkness without any strength of resistance. When permitted to rise again, they could not find the reason for their newest defeat. The divine mystery of the Incarnation in Mary's womb was concealed from Satan and his followers.

The Incarnation of the Word remains as mystery to our tainted human nature. The formation of Christ's body, the creation of the soul, and the union of the Divinity with the humanity, which was capable of suffering, all happened in the one same instant.

Mary prayed earnestly for guidance in her new position of being the Mother of the Onlybegotten of the Father. She was answered in these words: "My Dove, do not fear, for I will assist you and guide you, directing you in all things necessary for the service of my onlybegotten Son."

Her state of ecstasy, which held her while all this happened, came to an end, and Mary prostrated herself in adoration of the Divine Son, God and man, conceived in her virginal womb. In close imitation of Christ, Mary lived to share in his joys and sorrows. She always carried the sword in her loving mother heart, knowing that the prophecies of the passion, torments, ignominies and death of the Redeemer would be fulfilled — a sorrow which was hers without companionship or alleviation from any creatures.

Chapter 3

SHARING GOD'S SECRETS

Now that Mary was truly the Mother of the Messiah, there would be a change in her life. The Archangel Gabriel had included these words in his message to her:

> And behold, Elizabeth thy kinswoman also has conceived a son in her old age, and she who was called barren is now in her sixth month; for nothing shall be impossible with God (Luke 1:36,37).

In St. Luke's Gospel, it is also written that Zachary was offering incense in the Temple according to the laws of his priesthood, when an angel appeared to him and told him that his wife Elizabeth would bear a son, and that the child should be named John. The favor of the Lord would rest upon him, and he would be great, bringing many of the Israelites back to their God.

> And Zachary said to the angel, "How shall I know this? For I am an old man and my wife is advanced in years" (Luke 1:18).

> And the angel answered and said to him, "I am Gabriel, who stand in the presence of God; and I have been sent to speak to you and to bring you this good news. And behold, you shall be dumb and unable to speak until the day when these things come to pass, because

61

you have not believed my words, which will
be fulfilled in their proper time" (Luke
1:19,20).

A few days after the conception of Jesus, Mary was
inspired to visit her cousin Elizabeth.

Now in those days Mary arose and went with
haste into the hill country, to a town of Juda
(Luke 1:39).

When Mary told St. Joseph about this desire, he agreed
that it would be good. Without delay he bought food for
the four-day journey: fruit, bread, and a few fishes. He
also borrowed a beast of burden to carry Mary and their
provisions. When all was ready they departed for the home
of Zachary and Elizabeth. It was the will of God that the
Prophet and Precursor of Christ, St. John the Baptist,
should be sanctified before his birth by the presence of
the Savior.

Joseph was very loving and tried to do everything possible to make the journey comfortable for Mary. At times
when the terrain was smooth, Mary enjoyed walking. The
angels of Mary's guard accompanied them, being visible
only to her. It was not yet time for Joseph to know about
Mary's holy pregnancy. She knew the time would come
when it could no longer be concealed, and she realized
the great distress which would come to him when it became
so visible. Mary did not tell him, but prayed that the Lord
would make it known to him in his own way. Their conversations along the way included the subjects of the salvation of souls, the mercies of the Lord, and the coming
of the Redeemer.

Elizabeth had been told in a vision that Mary was on
her way to visit her. When she and Joseph arrived at the
house, Elizabeth with a few of her family welcomed them.

Mary said, "The Lord be with you, my dearest cousin."
Elizabeth answered, "The same Lord reward you for having come in order to afford me this pleasure." When they
were together alone, the words recorded in St. Luke's
Gospel were spoken:

> "Blessed are you among women and blessed
> is the fruit of your womb! And how have I
> deserved that the mother of my Lord should
> come to me? For behold, the moment that the
> sound of your greeting came to my ears, the
> babe in my womb leapt for joy. And blessed
> is she who has believed, because the things
> promised her by the Lord shall be accom-
> plished."

> And Mary said, "My soul magnifies the Lord,
> and my spirit rejoices in God my Savior;
> because he has regarded the lowliness of his
> handmaid; for, behold, henceforth all gener-
> ations shall call me blessed; because he who
> is mighty has done great things for me, and
> holy is his name. . . ." (Luke 1:42-49).

> And Mary remained with her about three
> months and returned to her own house (Luke
> 1:56).

The voice of Mary was God's instrument in bringing
the great blessings and extraordinary gifts to the child
John in Elizabeth's womb. In the sixth month of his conception his body was already in a state of natural perfection, yet his soul was in the state of original sin like
all others. In the womb of Mary, Jesus prayed to the Father
for all the highest graces to be bestowed upon the infant
John who was to precede Him in the act of Redemption.

God gave to John the perfect use of reason, sanctified him from original sin and filled him with the Holy Spirit. Mary of Agreda writes: "At the same time the fortunate child, looking through the walls of the maternal womb as through clear glass upon the incarnate Word, and assuming a kneeling posture, adored his Redeemer and Creator, whom he beheld in most holy Mary as if enclosed in a chamber made of the purest crystal." He made acts of faith, hope, charity, worship, gratitude and humility. All his life he grew in this original sanctity.

Elizabeth was delighted to have the presence of Mary with her and offered all her household for the service of her heavenly cousin. There was a special room adapted as a quiet retreat for prayer, which Mary occupied during her visit. The Queen of humility at once offered to assist Elizabeth as a handmaid.

When Mary saw Zachary, she asked for his blessing as a priest of the Lord. She did not attempt to cure him in his affliction because she knew the origin of his dumbness; she only prayed for him.

After staying with them for three days, Joseph returned to Nazareth with the understanding that he would be notified when Mary was ready to go back to their home.

In the house of Elizabeth, Mary continued her exalted gift of prayer. She rose at midnight and was absorbed in highest contemplation with visions of the Divinity, and observed the daily growth of the Divine Babe within her. With prudence she gave to waking and sleeping the time best suited to the natural state of her body. The holy Mother conversed with the angels, asking their guidance and care. With Elizabeth she also had many holy conversations in which they spoke of the wonderful attributes of God and his love for his creatures.

Elizabeth asked Mary to sew and prepare the swaddling clothes and coverlets in which the infant John would be wrapped. This our Lady did with loving hands. Mary also spent some of her time in manual occupations which her great humility led her to perform. In all ways she tried to truly be a handmaid to her cousin Elizabeth. Each of them wanted to serve the other.

Mary was so loving, gentle and kind that all hearts in Elizabeth's household were drawn to her. She did not fail to obtain many blessings for them.

The remaining days before the birth of St. John were quickly going by. St. Elizabeth wished that Mary would remain with her always. The spiritual benefits which came with Mary's presence were a source of continuous joy. The infant John had been enlightened beyond all other men born of women. After praying to learn the will of God, both mothers knew that their enjoyable companionship was coming to an end.

The joyful day of John's birth arrived. The holy child prayed for God's protection in entering a world with so many dangers to a human soul. Mary held the perfectly formed infant in her arms as he invited her tender caresses. She fondled him, but saved her kisses for only the Baby Jesus.

On the eighth day friends and relatives gathered for the rite of circumcision. They wanted the infant to have his father Zachary's name, but we learn in Luke's Gospel that Elizabeth said, "Not so, but he shall be called John." They asked what his father would have him named, and Zachary wrote on a tablet, "John is his name."

> And immediately his mouth was opened and his tongue loosed, and he began to speak, blessing God. And fear came on all their neighbors; and all these things were spoken abroad in all the hill country of Judea. And all who heard them laid them up in their heart, saying, "What then will this child be? For the hand of the Lord was with him" (Luke 1:64-66).

> And the child grew and became strong in spirit;
> and was in the deserts until the day of his
> manifestation to Israel (Luke 1:80).

In Mary of Agreda's writing we read that it was through the intercession of Mary that Zachary regained his ability to speak, and he died ten months later.

Chapter 4

THE SECRET REVEALED
TO ST. JOSEPH

The holy couple, Mary and Joseph, made the return journey to Nazareth very much like the way in which they had traveled to Judea. In one of the taverns they saw a woman who was very ill and depressed. Mary was shown the state of her soul. This unfortunate person was possessed by the demons. They had seen the former goodness of her actions, tempted her to sin and then became more powerful in their attempts to control her in body and soul. The Blessed Virgin Mary begged Christ to restore her to health. She commanded the devils to leave this poor creature and never return again. Good health was restored, and spiritual blessings were given to her through Mary's intercession. Other miracles were also performed by Mary on her way to her home in Nazareth.

The demons were again hurled into the infernal dungeons through the power of the Mother of God. Of course, this made Lucifer more furious than ever. He exclaimed: "Who is this weak woman, that commands us and oppresses us with so much power? What new surprise is this, and how can my pride stand it? We must hold a council and see how we can unite to destroy her." The fury of Satan was not abated. He organized his fellow demons into forces of the seven capital sins: pride, avarice, envy, wrath, lust, gluttony and sloth. Each of their attempts found no way to make Mary even listen to them in their deceitful flatteries with which they had gained success in leading others into sin. They were completely defeated.

Mary warns us to resist these temptations in their beginnings and trust that God will let no spiritual harm come upon us if we ask for her intercession and trust in her Divine Son. We also should remember the good angels appointed to protect us. They obey Mary as their immaculate Queen.

Our thoughts now follow St. Joseph as he becomes aware of Mary's pregnancy and is overwhelmed with anxiety, knowing that he had no part in it.

Our Spanish mystic writes: "The man of God was wounded to his inmost heart by an arrow of grief, unable to ward off the force of evidence, which at the same time wounded his soul. The principal cause of his grief was the most chaste, and therefore the most intense love with which he cherished his most faithful spouse, and in which he had from the beginning given over to her his whole heart." Both he and his holy spouse had promised to keep their vows of chastity, and he could find no fault in Mary's modest and pure behavior; yet he could not deny what was so evident to his eyes.

Mary knew all the thoughts of Joseph, and she was full of tenderness and compassion in his sufferings, serving him with more loving solicitude; yet she did not tell the source of her pregnancy. Mary did not feel free to disclose her mystery as she was still waiting for the command of God, and resigning it all into the hands of divine Providence.

Joseph could not bear the thought of having this matter brought to public attention, in which case the law would demand the stoning of an adulteress. After many weeks of anxiety and distress, the state of his health was weakening. Mary of Agreda writes: "There is no doubt that all this was one of the greatest trials not only of St. Joseph, but of the Princess of heaven and that it greatly manifested the most profound humility and wisdom of her most holy soul. The Lord thereby gave her an opportunity of exercising and proving all her virtues; for He had not only not commanded her to conceal the sacrament of her pregnancy, but contrary to his usual manner of proceeding, He had not even manifested to her his pleasure in any way."

St. Joseph decided that the best thing for him to do was to leave Mary and go to a place where he was unknown. He planned to leave that very night, packed some clothes and other trifles into a small bundle, claimed some wages due to him for his work, and then retired to rest with the intention of leaving at midnight. God allowed Mary to know the intentions of her spouse, and she prayed ardently that He would not leave her alone without a companion and protector.

It was during his sleep that the angel appeared to Joseph in a dream and gave him the message recorded in the Gospel of St. Matthew. The ways of the Lord are beyond our human comprehension.

> Now the origin of Christ was in this way. When Mary his mother had been betrothed to Joseph, before they came together, she was found to be with child by the Holy Spirit. But Joseph her husband, being a just man, and not wishing to expose her to reproach, was minded to put her away privately. But while he thought on these things, behold, an angel of the Lord appeared to him in a dream, saying, "Do not be afraid, Joseph, son of David, to take to thee Mary your wife, for that which is begotten in her is of the Holy Spirit. And she shall bring forth a son, and you shall call his name Jesus; for he shall save his people from their sins." Now all this came to pass that what was spoken by the Lord through the prophet might be fulfilled: "Behold, the virgin shall be with

child, and shall bring forth a son; and they
shall call his name Emmanuel," which is inter-
preted, "God with us" (Matt. 1:18-23).

Ven. Mary writes: "His Majesty so ordained events,
that both most holy Mary and St. Joseph should be brought
to the utmost reach of interior sorrow." It is not easy to
explain the new feelings of St. Joseph after this message
from the angel. I shall quote part of paragraph number
403 of this second volume of CITY OF GOD.

"Saint Joseph awoke with the full consciousness, that
his Spouse was the true Mother of God. Full of joy on
account of his good fortune and of his inconceivable happiness, and at the same time deeply moved by sudden
sorrow for what he had done, he prostrated himself to the
earth and with many other humble, reverential and joyful tokens of his feelings, he performed heroic acts of
humiliation and of thanksgiving. He gave thanks to the
Lord for having revealed to him this mystery and for having made him the husband of Her, whom God had chosen for his Mother, notwithstanding that he was not worthy
to be even her slave. Amid these recognitions and these
acts of virtue, the spirit of St. Joseph remained tranquil
and apt for the reception of new influences of the Holy
Spirit. His doubts and anxieties of the past few months
had laid in him those deep foundations of humility, which
were necessary for one who should be entrusted with the
highest mysteries of the Lord; and the remembrance of
his experiences was to him a lesson which lasted all his
life."

Joseph prayed for the grace and strength to ask forgiveness from his beautiful Spouse. A part of his prayer
is included: "Assist me, most powerful King, to make
some kind of reparation. I will go to my Spouse and Lady,
confiding in her sweetness and clemency; prostrate at her
feet I will ask her pardon, so that for her sake, You, my

eternal Lord and God, may look upon me with the eyes of a Father and may pardon my gross error." With tears in his eyes, he unwrapped the small bundle which he had planned to take with him at midnight. With new reverence and love, he prepared to approach the oratory where Mary awaited him.

When the hour came for the ending of Mary's contemplation, Joseph entered her room with greater reverence than he had ever felt before. He knelt in her presence, adoring the Infant Jesus living in her womb. He spoke words similar to these: "My Mistress and Spouse, true Mother of the eternal Word, here am I your servant prostrate at the feet of your clemency. For the sake of your God and Lord whom you bear in your virginal womb, I beseech you to pardon my audacity." Joseph wanted to be her faithful servant in every way for all the remaining years of his life. But Mary, with her deep love of humility, insisted that he continue to treat her as before, allowing her to do the household tasks and serve him as her superior.

These beautiful writings about Mary are quoted again: "She was all aflame in ecstasy and was raised from the earth in a globe of light, which surrounded her and transfigured her with the gifts of glory. At this heavenly vision St. Joseph was filled with admiration and unspeakable delight; for never had he seen his most blessed spouse in such eminence of glory and perfection. Now he beheld her with a full and clear understanding, since all the integrity and purity of the Princess of heaven and mystery of her dignity manifested themselves to him."

Ven. Mary also writes: "The Lord looked upon him in benevolence and kindness as upon no other man, for He accepted him as his foster-father and conferred upon him that title. In accordance with this dignity, He gifted him with that plenitude of science and heavenly gifts which Christian piety can and must acknowledge."

As revealed to her, Ven. Mary of Agreda writes more pages to describe the sheltered life of Mary and Joseph, as they awaited the time for the birth of Jesus. Now the holy couple could converse more openly about the Messiah and the mysteries of God contained in the Scriptures. Actually, Mary was the teacher, but she did it in a most humble manner, encouraging Joseph in a deeper understanding of a holy life. At times, Joseph was given the special favor of seeing the infant God in Mary's womb as enclosed in a ball of clearest crystal. Other times he saw Mary in ecstasy raised from the earth in brilliant light, or conversing with the angels; and sometimes prostrate on the earth in the form of a cross in prayer. He was privileged also to hear celestial music as the angels sang to their Queen, and he perceived a heavenly fragrance which filled him with great joy of spirit.

Their humble abode contained three rooms which occupied most of its space. One room was the bedroom of St. Joseph, another was his work place, and the third, that of Mary. Her resting place was a low couch made by St. Joseph, and on it were the coverings for her brief and holy slumber. She did not leave the dwelling except for urgent causes, and many times a neighbor performed the errands for her. In return, Mary procured many heavenly blessings for this woman and her family.

We also read about Mary's clothing. She wore an undergarment of soft cotton which no one else ever saw. Her outer tunics were gray in color. These and her veils were the only garments she changed now and then. "Not because they were soiled, but because, being visible to all, she wished to avoid notice by such strange sameness of outward appearance. Nothing that she wore upon her most pure and virginal body became soiled or worn."

There were times when the holy couple experienced real poverty, actually being without some of life's necessities. They were most generous in their gifts to the poor, and did not store up beforehand food or clothing. Both of them did work for others, but they did not ask for wages or set a price on their work. They gratefully accepted whatever their employers would give them. There were days when divine Providence provided food in various ways. Sometimes neighbors or acquaintances were inspired to bring a gift or pay a debt. More ordinarily St. Elizabeth sent a gift which Mary acknowledged by sending in return some work of her hands.

One day they were without any food at all. They prayed until very late, thanking God for this privation and trusting in his all-powerful hand. When they came from their separate rooms they found this surprise ready for them on the table. Angels had prepared a meal consisting of fruit, white bread, fishes and a sweet, nourishing preserve. They ate with fervent gratitude and sang songs of praise to our mighty God.

We quote again from Ven. Mary's writing: "Many other similar events came to pass almost daily in the house of most holy Mary and her spouse; for as they were alone and as there was no need of hiding these wonders from witnesses, the Lord did not hesitate to perform them for his beloved, who were entrusted with co-operation in the most wonderful of all the works of his powerful arm."

Chapter 5

THE DIVINE BIRTH
IN BETHLEHEM

We now come to the Christmas story as it has been portrayed in so many ways throughout the world. As St. Luke writes:

> Now it came to pass in those days, that a decree went forth from Caesar Augustus that a census of the whole world should be taken. This first census took place while Cyrinus was governor of Syria. And all were going, each to his own town, to register.
>
> And Joseph also went from Galilee out of the town of Nazareth into Judea to the town of David, which is called Bethlehem — because he was of the house and family of David — to register, together with Mary his espoused wife, who was with child. And it came to pass while they were there, that the days for her to be delivered were fulfilled. And she brought forth her firstborn son, and wrapped him in swaddling clothes, and laid him in a manger, because there was no room for them in the inn (Luke 2:1-7).

Mary, being a very prudent mother, had begun to prepare the swaddling clothes and coverlets for the divine Infant. She had already woven a piece of linen which

74

could be used for the swaddling wrappings. She had begun this weaving when they first began living in Nazareth, with the intention of giving it to the Temple in Jerusalem. Now it could be used for a greater purpose. She had asked St. Joseph to procure some woolen cloth of a soft texture and modest color for other coverings. Both Mary and Joseph prayed for heavenly guidance in all these activities. They heard the Lord's answer: "I have come from heaven to the earth in order to exalt humility and discredit pride, to honor poverty and contemn riches, to destroy vanity and establish truth, and in order to enhance worthily the value of labor. Therefore it is my will that exteriorly you treat Me according to the humble position which I have assumed, as if I were the natural child of both of you, and that interiorly you acknowledge Me as the Son of my eternal Father, and bestow the reverence and love due to Me as the Man-God."

In exchange for his work, Joseph accepted two pieces of woolen cloth, the one white, the other mulberry-colored mixed with gray. Mary used these to make the other necessary coverings for the Infant. Joseph also found a few flowers and herbs from which Mary extracted fragrant essences and with them she sprinkled the infant garments, laying them away in a small chest to be taken with her on their unexpected journey.

Mary's preparation for the birth of the Christ Child was not centered only on material things, but also on what is spiritual.

Quoting words from the second volume of Mary of Agreda's revelations: "The sovereign Queen understood better than all the rest of creation the ineffable greatness of the mystery of the Incarnation of a God and of his coming into the world. . . . She offered up the sacrifice of her burning love, and ransacked all the holy writings for hymns, canticles and psalms to praise and magnify this mystery, adding thereto the expression of her own exalted sentiments. In a mystical and yet altogether real manner she fulfilled the ancient figures and types by her virtues and by her interior and her exterior acts. She called upon and invited all the creatures to praise their God, to give honor and glory to their Creator, and place the hope of their sanctification in his coming into the world. In many of these exercises the most fortunate and blessed Joseph, her spouse, took part."

While Joseph was on an errand he heard that the Roman Emperor had issued an edict calling for a census of all the persons living in his domain. This would require each citizen to register in his own native town; Joseph would need to travel to Bethlehem, the town of David. He was not very happy when he told this to Mary. In prayer they were assured that it was the will of God for her to accompany him.

Mary was not completely surprised about going to Bethlehem because she knew the prophecies contained in Holy Scripture. However, she did not mention this to Joseph.

> But you, Bethlehem-Ephrata too small to be
> among the clans of Juda, from you shall come
> forth for me one who is to be ruler in Israel;
> whose origin is from of old, from ancient times.
> (Therefore the Lord will give them up, until
> the time when she who is to give birth has
> borne, and the rest of his brethren shall return
> to the children of Israel) (Micah 5:1,2).

This immutable decree was fulfilled and secured by the Lord through the edict of Caesar Augustus.

> You know, O Lord, that man is not master
> of his way; man's course is not within his
> choice, nor is it for him to direct his step (Jer.
> 10:23).

There would be many hardships in this five-day journey in midwinter, but they were ready to accept all difficulties in holy patience and joy. After much searching, Joseph was able to find an unpretentious little beast to carry Mary and the few provisions which their poverty could afford. The taverns where they spent the nights were crowded and noisy, and they were given the most undesirable places to rest. However, God certainly did not abandon his chosen ones. In addition to the angels already appointed for Mary's guard, others also were sent to provide heavenly light and spiritual joy along their way.

It was about four o'clock when our holy travelers arrived at their destination and twilight was already beginning, as it was the time of the winter solstice. Joseph had been very hopeful that they could spend the night at an inn or the house of a distant relative, but they were refused admittance. In their searching they passed the office of public registry, where they stopped to inscribe their names and pay the required fiscal tribute. Then continuing their quest to find lodging, they were met with refusals everywhere.

Joseph was filled with disappointment and heartrending sorrow. Then he remembered there was a cave outside the city walls, which was used as a shelter for shepherds and their flocks. Mary, who knew that Jesus came to teach the values of poverty, assured Joseph that such a place would be most satisfactory.

As Mary of Agreda writes: "Most holy Mary and saint Joseph entered the lodging thus provided for them and by the effulgence of the ten thousand angels of their guard they could easily ascertain its poverty and loneliness, which they esteemed as favors and welcomed with tears of consolation and joy. . . . It was formed entirely of the bare and coarse rocks, without any natural beauty or artificial adornment; a place intended merely for the shelter of animals; yet the eternal Father had selected it for the shelter and dwelling place of his own Son."

They began to clean the floor and corners of the cave, and were assisted by the angels which were visible to Joseph, not only to Mary. Joseph started a fire and they sat near it in order to get warm, and then began eating their frugal supper with joy. As the night was far advanced, Mary urged Joseph to rest and sleep. He retired to a place near the entrance of the cave and began to pray. Immediately he was absorbed in ecstasy and was shown all that passed during that night, and remained in that extraordinary state until called by Mary.

Joseph had arranged the straw in the manger as best he could for the comfort and convenience of Mary, using some of their garments as a couch. As Mary knelt, new effects of divine power drew her in a singular ecstasy. Quoting Ven. Mary again: "The veil fell and she saw intuitively the Godhead itself in such glory and plenitude of insight, as all the capacity of men and angels could not describe or fully understand." In adoration before the throne of Divinity, she offered glory, thanksgiving and praise for herself and all creatures. She also prayed for guidance in caring for this divine Infant soon to come into our world. Mary remained in ecstasy and this beatific vision until regaining her senses, and felt the Infant God beginning to move in her virginal womb. This did not cause any pain as that which is felt by other mothers giving birth. Quoting again: "Her body became so spiritualized with the beauty of heaven that she seemed no more a human and earthly creature. Her countenance emitted rays of light, like a sun incarnadined, and shone in indescribable earnestness and majesty, all inflamed with fervent love. She was kneeling in the manger, her eyes raised to heaven, her hands joined and folded at her breast, her soul wrapped in the Divinity and she herself was entirely deified. In this position, and at the end of the heavenly rapture, the most exalted Lady gave to the world the Onlybegotten of the Father and her own, our Savior Jesus, true God and man, at the hour of midnight, on a Sunday, in the year of the creation of the world five thousand one hundred and ninety-nine (5199) which is the date given in the Roman Church, and which date has been manifested to me as the true and certain one." (If the reader questions this date, we should remember that scientific knowledge has progressed much since the seventeenth century.)

In a miraculous manner, the Infant Christ penetrated the virginal chamber, coming forth in all purity, beauty, refulgence and immaculateness, preserving untouched the complete virginity of holy Mary. The angels Michael and Gabriel received Him and presented the divine Child to his Mother. Jesus spoke these words: "Mother, become like Me." How beautifully Mary did just that as she received Him in profound humility and reverence. She called St. Joseph and he adored the Child in tears of joy. As he handed the wrappings and swaddling clothes to Mary, she wrapped the divine Son with reverence, devotion and tenderness, and laid him in the crib, as related by St. Luke. As God had planned, an ox ran up from the field and entered the cave, joining the ass which had carried Mary from Nazareth. The heavenly Queen commanded them to show reverence and adore their Creator, as they warmed him with their breath.

> An ox knows its owner, and an ass, its master's manger; but Israel does not know, my people has not understood (Isa. 1:3).

An angel was sent to limbo where the Patriarchs were waiting for the promised Redeemer. With the Prophets they were told the good news as prophesied by Isaiah:

> Therefore the Lord himself will give you this

sign: the virgin shall be with child, and bear
a son, and shall name him Emmanuel (Isa.
7:14).

Mary also commanded the angels to tell the news of
Christ's birth to her parents, Anne and Joachim. These
holy ones sent a return message to Mary, asking her to
praise and adore the divine Child in their names, which
Mary immediately did. Another angel was sent to Elizabeth and her son John. Quoting again from Ven. Mary's
writing: "The child which had been consecrated as his
Precursor was renewed interiorly with a spirit more
inflamed than that of Elias, causing new admiration and
jubilation in the angels themselves."

Other angels brought the news of the long-expected
Messiah to the prophetess Anne and the priests Simeon
and Zachary. Others among the just received certain divine
effects at the hour of the holy birth, feeling a new supernatural joy, but not knowing its source.

And there were shepherds in the same district
living in the fields and keeping watch over
their flock by night. And behold, an angel of
the Lord stood by them and the glory of God
shone round about them, and they feared
exceedingly.

And the angel said to them, "Do not be afraid,
for behold, I bring you good news of great
joy which shall be to all the people; for today
in the town of David a Savior has been born
to you, who is Christ the Lord. And this shall
be a sign to you: you will find an infant
wrapped in swaddling clothes and lying in a
manger." And suddenly there was with the
angel a multitude of the heavenly host prais-

ing God and saying, "Glory to God in the highest, and on earth peace among men of good will" (Luke 2:8-14).

The shepherds were chosen above all others who were living in that area on this blessed night. Were there certain reasons for that choice? In CITY OF GOD it is written that they were unsophisticated and humble, being of sincere and upright hearts, speaking and hoping for the promised coming of the Messiah. They were guided to the cave where they saw the Divine One of all ages, and their lives were changed by that encounter with the Infant God. For the remainder of their lives they were filled with spiritual graces and wonder.

The power of God in the coming of the Word misled the proud and arrogant Lucifer and his legions. They knew that the woman whom they had unsuccessfully persecuted gave birth to a child, but there was nothing grand or elegant in a bare shelter for animals. In their thoughts, a Messiah would come in regal splendor and power. That the Redeemer would be born in such humble and poor surroundings was beyond their limited demoniac imaginations. The virginity of Mary before and after the birth of her child was concealed from Satan; also the message of the angels to the shepherds, and the star guiding the Magi with their exalted purpose in coming to Bethlehem remained unknown to the evil powers. The identity of Christ as the Savior was an unanswered question for them until the actual Sacrifice on Calvary, when their great defeat was fully recognized.

During the time of remaining in the cave, Mary held the divine Child in her arms most of the day and night. At times she placed him in the arms of holy Joseph who was filled with reverential wonder and joy as he realized his great privilege of actually touching the true Son of God, the incarnate Word. Both Mary and Joseph were always aware of the reverence to be shown toward the divine One.

The blessed young Mother nourished, served, and cared for the Infant given to her with the utmost reverence and perfection.

> And when eight days were fulfilled for his circumcision, his name was called Jesus, the name given him by the angel before he was conceived in the womb (Luke 2:21).

Mary was filled with sorrowful, tender love, knowing the pain to be felt by her divine Son in this rite of circumcision according to the law of Moses. She spoke to our heavenly Father about her thoughts and desires that she, instead of her Child, would feel the pain caused by this first shedding of his blood for the redemption of sinful mankind. A part of the answer coming from the Most High is quoted: "You know beforehand, my Daughter, that you must reserve your Onlybegotten and Mine for this and other greater sufferings. Resign yourself then, to the shedding of his blood and willingly yield to Me the first fruits of the eternal salvation of men."

Mary answered in words like these: "Supreme Lord and God, I offer to You this Victim and Host of acceptable sacrifice with all my heart, although I am full of compassion and sorrow that men (and women) have offended your immense goodness in such a way as to force a God to make amends."

Mary then spoke to Joseph about the necessary preparations. She said that she would hold the Child during the performance of this rite. She asked Joseph to obtain a glass vessel to preserve this sacred relic of the divine Infant, and prepared some linen cloths to catch the sacred blood.

Angels appeared in the presence of both Mary and Joseph with escutcheons bearing the name JESUS in beauty and glory. Among them were Michael and Gabriel in greater splendor and light than the others. They said, "Lady, this is the name of your Son, which was written in the mind of God from all eternity and which the Blessed Trinity has given to your onlybegotten Son and our Lord as the signal of salvation for the whole human race. . . ."

Bethlehem, like other towns of Israel, had its own synagogue for the worship of the people with a priest conducting the services. The sacrificial ceremonies, however, were reserved for the Temple in Jerusalem. Joseph requested the priest in Bethlehem to go with him to the cave where Mary was waiting with the holy Child in her arms for the ceremony of circumcision. Two attendants accompanied him. On entering the cave, the priest was slightly surprised at the poverty of the place, but when he saw the modesty and majestic graciousness of Mary, the Child's mother, he felt a sense of sacred mystery. Mary asked that he be very gentle in the procedure, and requested permission to hold the Child herself. She unwrapped the swaddling cloth and held a piece of linen so that the sacred flesh and blood would be caught in it.

We quote Mary of Agreda: "At the same time the Son of God, with immeasurable love, offered up to the eternal Father three sacrifices of so great value that each one would have been sufficient for the redemption of a thousand worlds. The first was that He, being innocent and the Son of the true God, assumed the condition of a sinner by subjecting Himself to a rite instituted as a remedy for original sin, and to a law not binding on Him. The second was his willingness to suffer the pains of circumcision, which He felt as a true and perfect man. The third was the most ardent love with which He began to shed his blood for the human race, giving thanks to the eternal Father for having given Him a human nature capable of suffering for his exaltation and glory."

Do not think that I have come to destroy the
Law or the Prophets. I have not come to
destroy, but to fulfill (Matt. 5:17).

Like other children, the divine Infant shed tears; not
only from the pain caused by the knife of flint, but even
more, in the supernatural sorrow caused by his knowledge of the hard-heartedness of mortals.

Mary, so tender and affectionate, also shed tears in this
suffering of the most holy One. The soothing medicine
was applied, and the divine Child was again wrapped in
the swaddling clothes. When asked for the chosen name
for the Infant, the parents answered: "JESUS is his name."
This was inscribed in the register with the names of other
children. While writing this name, the priest felt great
interior movements, and said, "I am convinced that this
Child is to be a great Prophet of the Lord. Have great
care in raising him, and tell me in what I can relieve your
needs." Mary and Joseph answered him with humble gratitude as the priest left their poor dwelling.

Ven. Mary of Agreda writes that the relics of the sacred
particle of flesh and the blood were then enclosed in the
crystal vase which Joseph had purchased with some of
the money sent by St. Elizabeth. The opening of the vase
was encased with silver, and Mary tightly sealed it with
a command. This was treasured by Mary during all her
life, and then entrusted to the Apostles — an inheritance
to the holy Church.

During the days of the wound's healing, Mary was more
solicitous than ever in her care for her divine Child. She
nourished him with her pure virginal milk three times a
day, asking his permission, and feeling that she was not
worthy of this.

The holy Infant gave her signs of endearment, placing
his baby arms around her neck, and welcoming her kisses
and caresses.

Mary of Agreda writes: "In all these things she behaved most perfectly and prudently, without defect or excess of any kind; the more openly and affectionately her most holy Son manifested his love toward her, so much the more deeply did she humiliate herself, and so much the greater was her reverence."

Mary, because of her infused knowledge of holy Scripture and supernatural enlightenment, knew that the Magi Kings of the Orient would come to Bethlehem to offer their adoration to this one true God. St. Joseph had suggested that they now could leave the cave and occupy a house which would be more convenient. While discussing this matter, the two angels Michael and Gabriel spoke to them with these words: "Divine Providence has ordained that three kings of the earth, coming from the Orient in search of the King of Heaven should adore the divine Word in this very place."

> The kings of Tharsis and the Isles shall offer gifts; the kings of Arabia and Saba shall bring tribute (Ps. 71:10).

The angels continued: "They are already ten days on the way; for at the hour of the birth of Jesus they were informed of it, and they immediately set out on their journey. Therefore they will shortly arrive, fulfilling all that the prophets had from very ancient times foreknown and foretold."

Balaam's prophesy:

> I see him, though not now; I behold him though not near: A star shall advance from Jacob, and a staff shall rise from Israel (Num. 24:17).

The three Magi Kings were mutual friends, natives of Persia, Arabia and Saba. Each of their kingdoms, being small, enabled them to govern with their own noble virtues, prudence and justice. They were learned in the natural sciences and in the Scriptures of God's chosen people, the Jews. On the night of Christ's birth, each was informed by an angel that the promised Messiah had come. The next day each prepared provisions with camels and a few servants for making the journey to the neighboring country of Palestine. A star appeared in the sky, different from other stars, and it was in a position to be seen by each of the kings in his own country. In following the star, the three met in one place at the same time, each with the same purpose of finding the Messiah and offering their adoration and the gifts they had chosen. With spiritual enlightenment one had selected gold; another, incense, and the third, myrrh. In following the star, they were guided to the city of Jerusalem.

> Now when Jesus was born in Bethlehem of Judea, in the days of King Herod, behold, Magi came from the East to Jerusalem, saying, "Where is he that is born king of the Jews? For we have seen his star in the East and have come to worship him." But when King Herod heard this, he was troubled, and so was all Jerusalem with him (Matt. 2:1-3).

When seeking information about the mysterious birth, Herod learned from the chief Priests and Scribes that the prophet Micah had indicated Bethlehem as the birthplace of the future king (Mic. 5:1).

> Then Herod summoned the Magi secretly, and carefully ascertained from them the time when the star had appeared to them. And sending them to Bethlehem, he said, "Go and make careful inquiry concerning the child, and when

you have found him, bring me word, that I
too may go and worship him" (Matt. 2:7,8).

The star reappeared to the three Kings, going before
them to Bethlehem until it rested over the place where
the infant King was waiting in the arms of Mary.

The star became smaller at the entrance of the cave,
shone brightly over the head of the holy Child, and then
disappeared. Joseph stood by the side of Mary, his spouse.
The Kings knew that Mary was a virgin, as had been
revealed in their study of the Scriptures.

Quoting words of this beautiful passage of CITY OF
GOD: "The heavenly Mother awaited the pious and devout
kings, standing with the Child in her arms. Amid the humble and poor surroundings of the cave, in incomparable
modesty and beauty, she exhibited at the same time a
majesty more than human, the light of heaven shining in
her countenance. Still more visible was this light in the
Child, shedding through the cavern effulgent splendor,
which made it like a heaven."

When entering, the three kings were overwhelmed in
wonder. In a prostrate position they adored the Infant as
true God and man, the Savior of our race. They wanted
to honor the holy Mother by kissing her hand, as was the
custom for the Queens in their own countries. However,
Mary offered the hand of Jesus instead, encouraging them
to realize their great privilege of being chosen to see what
other kings and prophets had only hoped to do.

After enjoying their time of spiritual enlightenment with
the holy family, the kings found lodging in the town of
Bethlehem. For several hours they discussed their experiences of that day and were blessed with burning love
in their hearts. During their sleep they were told to avoid
another encounter with Herod, and to return to their own
countries by another route. They returned to the cave and
presented the gifts which they had brought with them;

The most important ones were the gold, incense and myrrh. (Mary instructs us to offer our love as the gold; continual prayer as the incense; and the acceptance of labors and mortifications as the myrrh in our journey of life.)

The kings presented a few other gifts to relieve the poverty which they had seen. Precious jewels also were offered to Mary, but these she graciously refused. When ready to begin the return journey to their countries, the star again appeared and guided them on their way. The blessings of Bethlehem remained with them all their lives and these blessings were shared with the loyal subjects of their kingdoms.

Chapter 6

PRESENTATION IN THE TEMPLE

After the departure of the Kings, Mary informed Joseph that she would like to distribute the gifts from these royal men to others, keeping nothing for herself. They agreed to give the incense and myrrh, and also a portion of the gold to the Temple in Jerusalem; another part to the priest, who had circumcised the Infant, to be used for the Bethlehem synagogue and for his own priestly necessities. What was left, they would distribute among the poor. One poor and devout woman, who lived in a house near the gates of Bethlehem, invited them to stay with her. Mary and Joseph gratefully accepted, and gave her some of the gold which had been kept for distribution to the poor. They decided to live there until the time came for the ceremony of purification and the presentation of the holy Child in the Temple at Jerusalem.

The Christ Child had begun to speak to Mary at the time of his birth when they were alone, saying words like these: "Imitate Me, my chosen one; become like Me." This Mary did in every beautiful way. Ven. Mary writes: "Among the more rare and excellent privileges of most pure Mary, the chief one is, that she is Mother of God, which is the foundation of all the rest. The second is, that she was conceived without sin. The third, that she enjoyed many times the beatific vision in this mortal life, and the fourth is that she continually saw clearly the most holy soul of her Son and all its operations for her imitation."

And when the days of her purification were

89

> fulfilled according to the Law of Moses, they
> took him up to Jerusalem to present him to
> the Lord — as it is written in the Law of the
> Lord, "Every male that opens the womb shall
> be called holy to the Lord" — and to offer a
> sacrifice according to what is said in the Law
> of the Lord, "a pair of turtledoves or two young
> pigeons" (Luke 2:22-24).

Mary knew that she was free from all sin, but it was
proper in the will of God that she should go through the
purification ceremony as all other women of Israel. Also
it was the Father's will that the infant Christ should present himself in the Temple. Mary asked Joseph for his
blessing in making the journey, and asked that he allow
her to travel on foot, carrying in her arms the precious
Child entrusted to her care.

Mary of Agreda adds this bit of information: "Our
Queen was accustomed, for the sake of modesty, to wear
shoes, which covered her feet and served as a sort of
stocking. They were made of a certain plant used by the
poor, and something like hemp or mallow, dried and woven
into a coarse and strong texture, which, though poor, was
yet cleanly and appropriate."

St. Joseph very humbly gave Mary his blessing, telling
her he agreed that it would be fitting for her to walk as
she desired. (Mary always wanted to practice the virtue
of humility by asking Joseph's permission for her actions.
Joseph too practiced the virtue of humility in feeling his
unworthiness to give a command or blessing to the Queen
of Heaven.)

He then placed on the ass the chest containing the
Infant's clothing and the gifts for their Temple offering,
and they began their journey to Jerusalem. As they traveled along, visible angels accompanied them.

On their way, they stopped at the cave to venerate that

sacred place which had been the scene of the greatest holy mysteries.

It was a very cold wintry day, and Mary commanded the elements to keep their Infant Creator warm but to let the cold winds be felt only by her. At this command, it was done, and the wind was changed to a soft and balmy air for the holy Child, but the coldness was not diminished for his Mother.

By divine inspiration, the priest Simeon and the holy matron Anne were made aware of the coming of the holy family to the Temple. The chief procurator of the temporal affairs of that holy place, was informed of the appearance of the travelers, and was told to meet them by the Temple gate leading out to Bethlehem. He was also to invite them to stay at his house while they remained in the royal city. Our travelers were grateful for this place to spend the night.

That evening Joseph brought the gifts of gold, incense and myrrh to the Temple and was careful to escape notice. On his way he procured the two turtledoves which would be the offering for the holy Child on the following day.

> And behold, there was in Jerusalem a man named Simeon, and this man was just and devout, looking for the consolation of Israel, and the Holy Spirit was upon him. And it had been revealed to him by the Holy Spirit that he should not see death before he had seen the Christ of the Lord. And he came by inspiration of the Spirit into the Temple. And when his parents brought in the child Jesus, to do for him according to the custom of the Law, he also received him into his arms and blessed God, saying, "Now thou dost dismiss your servant, O Lord, according to your word in peace; because my eyes have seen your salvation,

which you have prepared before the face of
all peoples; a light of revelation to the Gentiles, and a glory for your people Israel" (Luke
2:25-32).

Simeon told Mary words of sorrow to come:

"Behold, this child is destined for the fall and
for the rise of many in Israel, and for a sign
that shall be contradicted. And your own soul
a sword shall pierce, that the thoughts of many
hearts may be revealed" (Luke 2:34,35).

Ven. Mary writes: "At the moment when the priest
Simeon mentioned the sword and the sign of contradic-
tion, which were prophetical of the passion and death of
the Lord, the Child bowed its head. Thereby, and by many
interior acts of obedience, Jesus ratified the prophesy of
the priest and accepted it as the sentence of the eternal
Father."

This was noticed and understood by Mary. Sorrow began
to fill her heart. As in a mirror she saw what the future
would bring: "how her most holy Son was to be the stone
of stumbling, the perdition of the unbelievers, and the
salvation of the faithful; the fall of the synagogue and
the establishment of the Church among the heathens; she
foresaw the triumph to be gained over the devils and over
death, but also that a great price was to be paid for it,
namely the frightful agony and death of the Cross."

Mary also saw the rewarding glory of the souls of the
just. All this was contained in her lifelong memory.

St. Joseph also was given an understanding of this mystery of suffering, though not so deeply as revealed to
Mary.

St. Luke also writes about the Prophetess Anne:

And coming up at that very hour, she began
to give praise to the Lord, and spoke of him
to all who were awaiting the redemption of
Jerusalem (Luke 2:38).

The holy family remained in Jerusalem for a few days,
spending much time in the Temple absorbed in prayer.
Mary of Agreda writes these words spoken by Christ to
his Mother: "My dearest Mother, dry up your tears and
let your purest heart be expanded; since it is the will of
my Father, that I accept the death of the cross, I desire
that you be my companion in my labors and sufferings;
I long to undergo them for the souls, who are the works
of my hands made according to my image and likeness,
in order to make them partakers of my reign and of eternal life in triumph over my enemies. This is what you
yourself do wish in union with Me."

Chapter 7

MIRACULOUS HAPPENINGS IN EGYPT

Mary and Joseph had hoped to make a novena of nine days of prayer, but God's plans were otherwise. On the fifth day of prayer, in a vision, Mary heard these words from Divinity: "In order to save the life of your Son and raise him up, you must leave your home and your country, fly with him and your spouse Joseph into Egypt. . . . The journey is long, most laborious and most fatiguing; suffer it all for my sake; for I am, and always will be with you." She left the Temple in tears, without telling St. Joseph the cause of her sorrow.

> But when they (the Magi) had departed, an angel of the Lord appeared in a dream to Joseph, saying, "Arise, and take the child and his mother, and flee into Egypt, and remain there until I tell you. For Herod will seek the child to destroy him." So he arose, and took the child and his mother by night, and withdrew into Egypt, and remained there until the death of Herod; that what was spoken by the Lord through the prophet might be fulfilled: "Out of Egypt I called my son" (Matt. 2:13-15).

Joseph immediately informed Mary and she tenderly awakened the divine Infant who shed a few tears. Mary and Joseph asked for his blessing which he gave to them in a visible manner. Preparations for the journey were soon made. Their poor clothing was placed in the small chest and loaded on their beast of burden. They departed shortly after midnight, hastening on their way to Egypt.

It was quite natural that the parents of the holy Child were filled with a certain amount of anxiety, not knowing what might happen on such a long journey; where and when it might end, nor how they might be accepted in Egypt as total strangers.

They were comforted with the appearance of many angels who were to accompany them and light their way in the darkness.

Mary would have liked to stop for a brief visit to the cave of the Nativity, but the angels told her of the dangerous circumstances. People had been talking about the three Magi Kings and their mysterious visit; also recalling the words of Simeon and Anne; some saying that her Son is a prophet and she is the Mother of the Messiah. Herod was aware of all this and was determined to find her.

Mary also thought of her cousin Elizabeth and her child John. She knew they were in Hebron at that time and would have liked to stop there, but Joseph told her it would not be prudent for them to do so. With Joseph's permission, Mary sent an angel to Elizabeth with a message of warning to let her know about the plans of the wicked King Herod.

Elizabeth sent a servant who brought gifts of various provisions, money, and material for clothing the infant Jesus. Some of these things Mary would be sharing with others among the poor. This servant met them in Gaza, a town on the road from Palestine to Egypt, not far from the Mediterranean Sea. Mary and Joseph stayed in that place for two days so that Joseph and their beast of burden could rest from the fatigue experienced in their hasty departure from Jerusalem.

Quoting from Ven. Mary of Agreda again: "During the two days which they spent in that city the most pure Mary, in order to enrich it with great blessings, performed some wonderful deeds. She freed two sick persons from the danger of death and cured their ailments. She restored to another person, a crippled woman, the use of her limbs. In the souls of many, who met her and conversed with her, she caused divine effects of the knowledge of God and a change of life."

In the words of the Blessed Virgin Mary spoken to our Spanish mystic we find these: "I was particularly struck with wonder to see the most sacred humanity pray and beseech his eternal Father to confer upon Herod, at this very time, enlightenment, help and blessing; to see my Son, who had it so much in his power to punish him, by his prayers prevent the full measure of chastisement which he deserved."

We can imagine that the loving heart of Mary must have felt deep compassion for the mothers and babes in Bethlehem and the surrounding districts.

Our travelers suffered many inconveniences and hardships when they left Gaza and began their sixty-league journey through the sandy deserts of Bersabe. (A league is the distance of about three miles.)

Ven. Mary of Agreda describes only a few of their trials: ". . . they had no other night-shelter than the sky and open air; moreover, it was in the time of winter, for this journey took place in the month of February, only six days after the Purification. . . . In the first night on these sandy plains they rested at the foot of a small hill, this being the only protection they could find. . . . In order to furnish them with some kind of shelter against the open air, however narrow and humble it might be, Joseph formed a sort of tent for the divine Word and most holy Mary by means of his cloak and some sticks. . . . He slept upon the ground, resting his head upon the chest which contained the clothing and other articles of their baggage."

As they continued their journey, their small store of food was soon exhausted. Mary prayed for aid and ended a prayer in words such as these: "My Lord and Father, look upon your Onlybegotten and grant me what is necessary to sustain my natural life and also that of my spouse, so that I may serve your Majesty and your Word made flesh for the salvation of men."

Then angels brought delicious bread, well-seasoned fruits, and a tasty, nourishing drink. Together with the angels our travelers sang songs of praise and thanksgiving to the Lord.

Several times during their journey the angels constructed a brilliant globe around and over the holy three and thus protected them from some of the inclemencies of the weather during the cold nights.

A few times when Mary rested on the ground from her fatigue, a great number of birds came from the hills to entertain her, perching on her shoulders with signs of great joy. Ven. Mary writes: "The most prudent Queen gently received them and invited them to acknowledge their Creator by their songs and to be thankful for his having created them so beautiful and arrayed them in their gorgeous plumage, given them the air and the earth for their enjoyment, and provided them with daily food and sustenance. The birds responded to her exhortations with joyous movements and sweet warblings, while the loving Mother joined them with still more sweet and melodious songs for the infant Jesus, extolling and blessing him as her God and her Son, and as the Author of all these wonders. . . ."

In this way our exiles proceeded on their difficult way to Egypt.

Oracle on Egypt: See the Lord is riding on a swift cloud on his way to Egypt; the idols of Egypt tremble before him, the hearts of the

Egyptians melt within them (Isaiah 19:1).

The events written in this prophesy happened at the time of Christ's birth.

The reason for the flight into Egypt included more than only an escape from the cruelty of Herod. It gave the Infant God the opportunity to visit that country and to perform the miracles recorded by the ancient prophets. Being conducted by the angels, according to the decrees of the Most High, Jesus, Mary and Joseph were led through the populated parts of Egypt. This was done in a round-about way before arriving at their place of abode in Heliopolis, the city which was later named Cairo. Their roundabout journey in this way continued for more than fifty days, making the distance from Jerusalem a total of more than two hundred leagues. A more direct route could have been shorter.

In many places, including even the small villages, temples had been built for the worship of idols, all in the power of the demons from hell. Astonishing things began to happen.

When entering the towns, the incarnate Word, as the babe held in Mary's arms, used his divine power to free the Egyptians from their slavery to Satan. Like lightning the demons were forced to descend to the deepest caverns of hell. Ven. Mary writes: "At the same instant the idols crashed to the ground, the altars fell to pieces, and the temples crumbled to ruins. The cause of these marvelous effects were known to the heavenly Lady, for she united her prayers with those of her most holy Son as Co-operatrix of his salvation. Joseph also knew this to be the work of the incarnate Word; and he praised and extolled Him in holy admiration."

The demons were completely overcome and did not know the source of the divine power which again had hurled them into their deepest place of eternal torments.

The Egyptian people were amazed at what was happening. Some of the more learned citizens knew of the ancient tradition which said that a King of the Jews would come and that the temples of the idols would be destroyed. But the common people had no knowledge of this prophesy and the more learned did not know how or when it would happen. Therefore, terror and confusion was spread among the inhabitants as prophesied by Isaiah.

> The people who walked in darkness have seen
> a great light; upon those who dwelt in the
> land of gloom a light has shone (Isaiah 9:1).

Some of the people met Mary and Joseph. The virgin Mother used this opportunity to teach them about the one true God.

Quoting again: "The heavenly Lady was so sweet and kind in her words, and at the same time so full of life and force; her appearance was so charming, and all her intercourse was accompanied by such salutary effects, that the rumor of the arrival of these strange Pilgrims quickly spread about in the different towns, and many people gathered to see and hear them."

Ven. Mary writes about the demons in Heliopolis (Cairo). "One of them dwelt in a tree at the entrance to the city; for the neighboring inhabitants had begun to venerate this tree on account of its size and beauty, whence the demon had taken occasion to erect his seat in it. When the incarnate Word came within sight of this tree, not only was the demon hurled from his seat and cast into hell, but the tree bowed down to the ground, as if rejoiced at its good fortune; for even the senseless creatures testified how tyrannical is the dominion of the devil. . . . But the memory of this event remained for centuries, for the leaves and fruits of this tree cured many sicknesses."

Of course, Satan was infuriated beyond imagination.

He discovered that the presence of Mary seemed to be the reason for another great defeat; he did not suspect anything powerful in her infant Child. When he had organized his fellow demons for another attack on Mary, his great enemy, they had no ability to come nearer to her than a distance of two thousand paces. Again he was suddenly thrown into hell's abyss with all his squadrons and wicked spirits. He was totally confused — expecting the Messiah to come in great royal acclaim and majesty, not like a little babe still in the arms of his mother.

Chapter 8

A DWELLING IN HELIOPOLIS

Saint Joseph was able to find a suitable house just a short distance from the city. With borrowed instruments, Mary cleaned and arranged the poor little house with thanksgiving in her heart.

Now the miraculous assistance which they had received in their trip through the desert ceased, and Joseph found it necessary to beg for alms. "For so early the Lord of all creation allowed himself to fall into this extreme of being obliged to beg for his sustenance, in order that He might have an occasion to return the alms a hundredfold."

When Joseph was able to receive wages for his work, he made a couch for Mary and a cradle for Jesus. His own resting place was only the bare ground until he could make other necessary pieces of furniture for their convenience. The work of a carpenter was not always plentiful, and Mary began to help earn a livelihood by her exquisite weaving and needlework. She united prayer with her labors to obtain life's necessities.

The holy Infant gave her a rule for the schedule of her daily life: "My dearest Mother, from the time of nightfall, you shall take some sleep and rest. And from midnight until the break of day you may occupy yourself in contemplation with Me, and We will praise the eternal Father. Thereupon prepare the necessary food for yourself and Joseph; and afterwards give Me nourishment and hold Me in your arms until the third hour, when you shall place Me in the arms of your husband, in order to afford him some refreshment in his labors. Then retire until it is time to prepare his meal and return to your work." The holy Child also told Mary to follow him in perfect imitation. We are remembering that Mary had the special spiritual gift of seeing all that passed in the soul of the incarnate Word.

During their years of living in Egypt, many persons came to Mary and Joseph for help in their illnesses and spiritual hunger. Those in good faith were miraculously cured and inspired to live a holy life. Many offered presents to Mary, but she accepted only what might be appropriate to distribute to others living in poverty.

At this time Herod carried out his wicked plan.

> Then Herod, seeing that he had been tricked by the Magi, was exceedingly angry; and he sent and slew all the boys in Bethlehem and its neighborhood who were two years old or under, according to the time that he had carefully ascertained from the Magi. Then was fulfilled what was spoken through Jeremiah the prophet, "A voice was heard in Rama, weeping and loud lamentation; Rachel weeping for her children, and she would not be comforted, because they are no more" (Matt. 2:16-18).

Herod gave this command six months after the birth of Christ. Looking into the soul of her divine Son, Mary saw all that happened in Bethlehem.

"She saw also how her Son prayed to his eternal Father for the parents of these innocents; that He offered up the murdered children as the first fruits of his own Death; asking Him also that they receive the use of reason, in order that they might be a willing sacrifice for their Redeemer and accept their death for his glory."

All this sorrow was felt by Mary. She knew that John,

now in the care of Elizabeth, might also be in danger. Zachary had died about four months after the birth of Christ. Through an angel sent by Mary, Saint Elizabeth had received information about Herod's actions, and in order to save her son John she fled to the desert and hid in a cave. In much difficulty and hardship she was able to find sustenance for herself and the child. Quoting from paragraph 676 in Ven. Mary's writings: "The heavenly Lady also knew that saint Elizabeth, after three years of this solitary life, died in the Lord; that saint John remained in the desert, commencing to live an angelic life, and that he was not to leave his solitude until he should be commanded by the Almighty to preach penance as his Precursor. These sacraments and mysteries the Infant Jesus manifested to his most holy Mother with many other hidden and profound blessings conferred upon saint Elizabeth and her son in that desert."

Mary sent angels with provisions to help them with the hardships found in their wild abode. When John was four years old his mother died. Angels helped him to bury Elizabeth. Mary sent an angel to bring food to the child John until he was old enough to provide his own sustenance with herbs, roots and woodland honey. (Holy Scripture also mentions locusts as his food.)

> But John himself had a garment of camel's hair and a leathern girdle about his loins, and his food was locusts and wild honey (Matt. 3:4).

When the child Jesus was one year old, he spoke his first words to Joseph. (His speaking with Mary had begun at his birth.)

Mary also knew that this was the time to free him from the swaddling clothes and dress him in other garments for his divine person to wear. At his request, she wove a tunic of one piece without a seam. It had the color of a mixture of brown and silvery gray. She also wove a pair of sandals for his sacred feet. Jesus told her that when it was time for his public life to begin, he must be barefoot. His mother also made a half tunic of linen as an undergarment. All these pieces of clothing grew with his body, never became worn or soiled. The garment which Jesus laid aside at the Last Supper, when washing the feet of his Apostles, was a mantle or cape. This had been made by Mary after their return to Nazareth. Like the other clothing, it grew with the Lord and never became soiled or worn. Its color was like that of the tunic, being only a little darker.

Mary joined Jesus in all his prayers for the redemption of souls. She witnessed many things which were never known by others. At times the incarnate Word, as a child, prostrated himself on the ground, other times being raised in the form of a cross in prayer to the Father for the salvation of souls. Mary joined him in perfect imitation. Quoting again from the second volume of CITY OF GOD: "On these occasions it often happened that the Child Jesus in the presence of his most holy Mother wept and perspired blood, for this happened many times before his agony in the garden. Then the blessed Lady would wipe his face, interiorly perceiving and knowing the cause of this agony, namely the loss of the foreknown and of those who would be ungrateful for the benefits of their Creator and Redeemer and in whom the works of the infinite power and goodness of the Lord would be wasted. All these wonders commenced from the time when at the age of one year he began to walk, witnessed only by his holy Mother, whose heart was to be the treasure-house of his wonders."

The holy Child, with his parents, grew in the admiration and esteem of others in Egypt when they became acquainted, and all received spiritual benefits from the incarnate God.

But when Herod was dead, behold, an angel of the Lord appeared in a dream to Joseph in Egypt, saying, "Arise and take the child and his mother and go into the land of Israel, for those who sought the child's life are dead." So he arose and took the child and his mother, and went into the land of Israel. But hearing that Archelaus was reigning in Judea in place of his father Herod, he was afraid to go there; and being warned in a dream, he withdrew into the region of Galilee. And he went and settled in a town called Nazareth; that there might be fulfilled what was spoken through the prophets, "He shall be called a Nazarine" (Matt. 2:19-23).

This happened when Jesus was seven years old. Their return journey through the desert was much like it had been when they left Palestine, at certain times receiving necessities in miraculous ways. When arriving in Nazareth they found their house had been well cared for by a devout cousin of St. Joseph. Here they continued their lives of holiness and grateful obedience to the almighty Father.

THE TRANSFIXION

The Sacramental Mysteries of the Life of the Mother of God from the Return out of Egypt up to her Divine Son's Ascension into Heaven

THE TRANSFIXION

CONTENTS

Chapter 1

CELEBRATING FEAST DAYS IN JERUSALEM

And his parents used to go every year to Jerusalem at the Feast of the Passover (Luke 2:41).

Soon after the Holy Family had settled in Nazareth, it became the time of year for the Jews to present themselves in the Temple at Jerusalem. This obligation extended to three times a year, and was a duty binding only on the men. However, the women and children were free to go according as their devotion might inspire them.

Three times a year, then, every male among you shall appear before the Lord, your God, in the place which he chooses: at the feast of Unleavened Bread, at the feast of Weeks, and at the feast of Booths. No one shall appear before the Lord empty-handed, but each of you with as much as he can give, in proportion to the blessings which the Lord, your God, has bestowed on you (Deut. 16:16,17).

The feast of Unleavened Bread, was also known as the Passover or Pasch; the feast of Weeks was also known as Pentecost; and another name for Booths was Tabernacles.

It was decided that all three would make the journey to Jerusalem for the feast of the Pasch, while Joseph would go by himself for the other two prescribed feasts,

111

offering the gifts always saved for these occasions.

Mary of Agreda writes: "Many times, when the Child was fatigued and overheated, the loving and prudent Mother was moved to tenderest and tearful compassion. She inquired about his sufferings and fatigue and wiped his divine countenance, which was more beautiful than the heavens and all its stars. She used to do this on her knees and with ineffable reverence. The divine Child would respond with much pleasure and speak of the delight with which He accepted these hardships for the glory of the eternal Father and for the good of men."

On the way to Jerusalem Jesus and Mary performed works of charity for other souls, converting them in the knowledge of God, freeing them from sin, and leading them to practice virtue; but all this was done in a way to escape notice. The holy Mother also consulted her divine Son in regard to their stopping-places and lodging-houses along the way. Quoting again from the information given to Ven. Mary: "The heavenly Princess well knew that her Son pre-arranged the occasions for his admirable works, which He foresaw and fore-ordered in his wisdom."

Mary was gifted with the grace to see the soul of her holy Son as he prayed for the redemption of all in our human race. She saw in her mind all the suffering that Jesus would endure in the future. The sword mentioned by Simeon caused many tears in anticipation of the terrible torments and death of her precious divine Son.

> And the child grew and became strong. He was full of wisdom and the grace of God was upon him (Luke 2:40).

On the occasion of celebrating the feast of the Pasch, when Jesus was twelve years old, he remained behind in Jerusalem unknown to his parents who had begun their return journey to Nazareth.

And after they had fulfilled the days, when they were returning, the boy Jesus remained in Jerusalem, and his parents did not know it. But thinking that he was in the caravan, they had come a day's journey before it occurred to them to look for him among their relatives and acquaintances. And not finding him, they returned to Jerusalem in search of him (Luke 2:43-45).

We may wonder how it was possible that the child Jesus could escape the notice of his parents. Mary had been absorbed in divine contemplation, and when this spiritual experience ended, she thought that Jesus must be with Joseph. It was the custom for the men to make the journey in one separate group, and the women walked together in another group, making arrangements to meet at a certain place in the evening. The children accompanied either of their parents. When Mary and Joseph met at the place agreed upon, and discovered that Jesus was not with them, they were filled with surprise and misgivings. After inquiring about Jesus among their relatives and friends, they received no information about him. Mary confided in her angels, who had never lost sight of the incarnate Word, but according to God's plan, it was not yet time for them to reveal to her where he might be found.

In Mary's anxiety, she had many disturbing thoughts. She said to Joseph, "My spouse and my master, my heart cannot rest, unless we return with all haste to Jerusalem in order to seek my most holy Son."

Ven. Mary of Agreda tells this: "Not all the sorrows suffered by all the martyrs ever reached the height of the sorrows of most holy Mary in this trial; nor will the patience, resignation and tolerance of this Lady ever be equalled, nor can they; for the loss of Jesus was greater to her than the loss of anything created, while her love

and appreciation of Him exceeded all that can be conceived by any other creature."

We follow Mary in her quandary. Was it possible that
Archelaus, like the cruelty of his father Herod, could have
in some way obtained information about Jesus and had
taken him as a prisoner, even though the time for his Passion and Death had not yet come?

Could it be that she may have failed in some way in
her care for him, and that he had gone to live with his
precursor John in the desert? Her angels told her that he
was not there. Then she thought he might have gone to
Bethlehem and she might find him in the cave of the
Nativity, but the angels assured her he was not so far
away.

Our Spanish mystic tells that Mary did receive some
hopeful answers to her queries. In answer to Mary's description of Jesus, one woman told her: "This Child, with those
same marks, came yesterday to my door to ask for alms,
and I gave some to him; and his grace and beauty have
ravished my heart. And when I gave him alms, I felt
myself overcome by compassion to see a child so gracious in poverty and want." Other persons gave similar
answers of having seen her Beloved. Mary also learned
that Jesus had been seen in the city hospitals.

In the revelations made to Ven. Mary of Agreda we
read this: "It was very near to the gate of the city that
the divine Child turned and hastened back through the
streets. Foreseeing in his divine fore-knowledge all that
was to happen, he offered it up to his eternal Father for
the benefit of souls. He asked for alms during these three
days in order to ennoble from that time on humble men-
dicity as the first-born of holy poverty. He visited the
hospitals of the poor, consoling them and giving them the
alms which he had received; secretly he restored bodily
health to some and spiritual health to many, by enlightening them interiorly and leading them back to the way

of salvation. On some of the benefactors, who gave him alms, he performed these wonders with a greater abundance of grace and light; thus fulfilling from that time on the promise, which he was afterwards to make to his Church: that he who gives to the just and to the prophet in the name of a prophet, shall receive the reward of the just" (Matt. 10:41).

Then Mary heard words from the angels: "Our Queen and Lady, the hour of your consolation is at hand; soon you will see the Light of your eyes; hasten your footsteps and go to the Temple." At that moment Joseph met his spouse, for with the hope of finding Jesus more quickly, they had separated to go in different directions. He too had received a message from an angel. We quote from St. Luke:

> And it came to pass after three days, that they found him in the Temple, sitting in the midst of the teachers, listening to them and asking them questions. And all who were listening to him were amazed at his understanding and his answers. And when they saw him, they were astonished. And his mother said to him, "Son, why have you done so to us? Behold, in sorrow your father and I have been seeking you." And he said to them, "How is it that you sought me? Did you not know that I must be about my Father's business?" And they did not understand the word that he spoke to them. And he went down with them and came to Nazareth, and was subject to them; and his mother kept all these things carefully in her heart (Luke 2:46-51).

Jesus had gone to the Temple on the day when the rabbis had met to discuss some of the doubtful points of

Holy Scripture concerning the coming of the promised Messiah. Talk about the amazing occurrences in Bethlehem when the angels had lighted up the sky with their appearance and glorious singing, and the visit of the three kings seeking the new King of the Jews, had influenced some of them to believe that the Messiah was already in the world. Others in the group did not agree with them. These rabbis believed that the Messiah would come in great majesty and power, perhaps even freeing them from the dominion of Rome. This hope had not been realized. Jesus presented himself as a humble disciple, but wanting to make the truth known, he quoted from the prophecies concerning his coming.

"For Isaiah says, that He shall be our Law-giver and King, who shall save his people (Is. 30,27), and David, that he shall crush all his enemies (Ps. 94,3). Daniel, that all tribes and nations shall serve him (Dan. 7,14), Ecclesiasticus, that he shall come with a great multitude of the saints (Eclus. 24,3)."

Jesus continues: "But the doubt arises from the comparison of these with other passages in the Prophets, since all of them must be equally true. . . . Isaiah, "that He shall be satiated with reproach; that He shall be led as a sheep to the slaughter, and that He shall not open his mouth (Is. 53,8). Jeremiah states that the enemies of the Messiah shall join hands to persecute Him . . . (Jer. 11,19). David says that He shall be the reproach of the people, trodden under foot, despised as a worm (Ps. 21,78). Zachary, that He shall come meek and humble seated upon an insignificant beast (Zach. 9,9)."

Jesus explains how to reconcile these prophecies. The Messiah is to come twice to the world, first as its Redeemer, and secondly as its Judge.

Mary and Joseph entered at the time when Jesus was presenting his last argument. The teachers of the law were astounded at what they had heard from Wisdom itself, and their Treasure had been joyfully found by Mary and Joseph as St. Luke tells us.

Chapter 2

PREPARATION FOR BECOMING MOTHER AND TEACHER OF THE CHURCH

It is to be remembered that Christ spent only three years of his public life in choosing and instructing the twelve men selected as his apostles, while thirty years were spent in the company of the Blessed Virgin Mary, eighteen of them after his concealment in the Temple. Jesus carefully prepared Mary for her office as Teacher of the Church, which she would become after his Ascension to the eternal heavens.

In CITY OF GOD we read: "During all those years Mary alone was the disciple of Christ. In addition therefore to the ineffable gifts of grace and holiness, which he had conferred upon her until their arrival in Nazareth, he infused into her new light and made her a participant in his divine knowledge, depositing and engraving into her heart the whole law and doctrine of grace, which to the end of the world was to be dispensed by his holy Church. This was moreover effected in such an exalted manner that no human thought or words can express it; and the great Lady was thereby filled with such wisdom and knowledge, that it would suffice to enlighten many worlds, if there were more than one."

Divine enlightenment came in different ways to Mary: sometimes in abstractive visions which at this time of her life were more frequently received; other times in intellectual visions. These enabled her to have a deeper understanding of the Divinity and the place of Christ in its

118

mysteries. Mary was also privileged to see the soul of Jesus with its interior operations as in a mirror for her imitation. A fourth source of information was his spoken word concerning his Church in all the different phases of its existence and development. Jesus and Mary could also communicate in an interior way, reading each other's thoughts and sentiments.

Like writing on the tablet of her loving heart, Jesus explained in detail the mysteries of the new evangelical law which he had come to establish in his true Church on earth.

Mary was informed of all the teachings written in the four Gospels, having more knowledge than the writers themselves. In Mary of Agreda's words: "She comprehended the evangelical precepts, counsels and parables of the Gospel; as for instance, the precepts of loving enemies, pardoning injuries, doing good works in secret and without vainglory, avoiding hypocrisy; the counsels of perfection and the teachings contained in the parables of the recovered treasures, the lost pearl, the virgins, the seed scattered on the ground, the talents and all other parables of the four Gospels. All of them she understood, together with the doctrines which they inculcate, and the high ends which the Master had in view."

She knew and practiced in all their utmost perfection the Beatitudes given by Christ in his Sermon on the Mount as recorded by St. Matthew.

> Blessed are the poor in spirit, for theirs is the kingdom of heaven.
> Blessed are those who mourn, for they shall be comforted.
> Blessed are the meek, for they shall inherit the earth.
> Blessed are those who hunger and thirst for righteousness, for they shall be satisfied.

> Blessed are the merciful, for they shall obtain mercy.
>
> Blessed are the pure in heart, for they shall see God.
>
> Blessed are the peacemakers, for they shall be called sons of God.
>
> Blessed are those who are persecuted for righteousness' sake, for theirs is the kingdom of heaven.
>
> Blessed are you when men revile and persecute you and utter all kinds of evil against you falsely on my account. Rejoice and be glad, for your reward is great in heaven. (Matt. 5:3-12). (Catechism of the Catholic Church, 1716)

The Church teaches that these Beatitudes respond to the natural desire for happiness, which God has placed in the human heart.

All the articles of faith as professed by the Catholic Church in its Apostles' Creed and the Nicene Creed used at Mass were understood in a comprehensive and illuminating way by the Virgin Mary.

In visions, our Blessed Mother saw the whole militant Church in salvation history from the beginning of creation till the end of the world and in eternal beatitude. She received knowledge of the future saints who would accomplish the purpose for which they were created. They would serve the Catholic Church as Apostles, Martyrs, Doctors, Confessors and Virgins; also the other countless men, women and children who would accept and merit the joys of salvation. She was the most avid listener to the teachings of her son Jesus. Mary was also shown the souls who would be disdainful and who would refuse the saving graces offered to them. For these persons she shed many tears of sorrow.

Mary knew the importance of the Ten Commandments as given to Moses. They were designed by God for the happiness and salvation of all people in our human race — not only for the Hebrews who had escaped from their Egyptian slavery. The first three tell of our duties to God, and the last seven are to be followed in our activities with other people. Saint Matthew tells how they are summarized by Christ as the two Great Commandments: "You shall love the Lord your God with your whole heart, your whole soul, and your whole mind." and "You must love your neighbor as yourself" (Matt. 22:37-39). This second is called "The Golden Rule" professed and practiced by many people of different world faiths (Hinduism, Buddhism, Taoism, Confucianism, Judaism, Christianity, Islam). "Thou shalt love others as you love yourself." Mary's influence extends to those who do not even know her.

Mary was also made to know the Seven Sacraments and their benefits to mankind. Even at this early date, before its institution, she began to prepare for the reception of the Holy Eucharist. In her special love she tried to make atonement for those who would receive this most holy Sacrament unworthily and without reverence. She knew the importance of these Sacraments in our Catholic life. The first, Baptism, replaced the ancient rite of circumcision. Its form was to be pure natural water and the words to accompany it would include the names of the three Persons in the Blessed Trinity. This Sacrament would be powerful enough to remove all stain of sin, and would confer the strong virtues of faith, hope and charity, making its recipients true children of the Church.

Confirmation, with the use of holy oil and chrism, imprints a certain character on the soul as a strengthening of our faith. Mary saw the great benefits of the Sacrament of Penance (Reconciliation) and the necessity of it for our weak human nature. For the greatest of all the

Sacraments, Holy Eucharist, our Lady gave special thanks and praise to her Son, asking that as soon as possible after its institution, he would come to her heart in this form of bread.

Mary of Agreda writes these words as a promise of Christ to his holy Mother: "My beloved Mother, many times shalt thou receive Me in the holy Sacrament, and after my Death and Ascension into heaven that shall be thy consolation; for I shall choose thy most sincere and loving heart as my most delightful and pleasant resting-place." It is told that whenever Mary received the consecrated bread (truly the Body of Christ) it would remain in her heart until the next time she received this Sacrament; only then being consumed in the natural function of a human body. This would always happen with each new reception, making her heart to be a living Tabernacle for her holy Son.

In the early ages of the Catholic Church there was a Sacrament known as Extreme Unction. It is now known as Anointing of the Sick. This Sacrament gives strength to the soul in passing through its journey on earth to the beginning of what Christ has promised as our eternity of heaven. It is comforting to know the attacks of Satan at that final hour can be overcome. Illness and suffering are a part of life. Accepted in the Christian way, this Sacrament sometimes brings a restoration of health if that is good for the salvation of the person. These sufferings can always bring one closer to God. We can trust that our heavenly Queen will be with us in our final moments if we only think of her as leading us to Jesus.

The Sacrament of Holy Orders brought to Mary a great reverence for the priesthood. Quoting: "She understood how her most blessed Son, the provident Founder of grace and of the Church, thereby constituted apt ministers of his Sacraments for the sanctification of his mystical body and for the consecration of his Body and Blood; giving them a dignity above that of all men and of the angels themselves." Mary understood how the Sacrament of Matrimony was instituted to sanctify and bless men and women in their love for one another as they would cooperate in God's plan for the further continuance of our human race. It also was a type of the mystery of the spiritual marriage and close union of Christ with his Church. She was given knowledge of how the Church would develop and be governed in the future centuries.

We again quote Mary of Agreda's words concerning the blessed Virgin Mary: "Her knowledge was so clear and deep, that it comprehended everything and was never equalled by any other creature, nor can it be conceived in its full extent either in thought or words. Neither was there anything wanting that is necessary, nor was there anything added that was superfluous, nor did she ever mistake one thing for another, nor was she in need of discourse or inquiry in order to be able to explain the most hidden mysteries of the Scriptures, whenever such explanation was necessary in the primitive Church."

Chapter 3

LIFE IN THE HOLY HOUSE
OF NAZARETH

As the years went by and as Jesus grew older, he began to spend much of his time away from their home in visiting the poor and infirm, and bringing consolation to those in sorrow. Small miracles were performed in a secret way as he led those souls into the way of salvation and away from sin. Our Lady knew of these activities and gave her Son thanks for them.

In the oratory of Mary, which was a narrow and poorly furnished room, Jesus prayed for the salvation of all people in his Father's creation. Mary joined him in prayer, imitating his words and posture. Sometimes Christ prayed while in a kneeling position, sometimes prostrate on the floor in the form of a cross, and at other times Mary saw Jesus raised in glory as the three privileged apostles, Peter, James and John, saw him in the Transfiguration told by St. Matthew in the seventeenth chapter of his Gospel.

> Now after six days Jesus took Peter, James and his brother John, and led them up a high mountain by themselves, and was transfigured before them. And his face shone as the sun, and his garments became white as snow (Matt. 17:1,2).

Mary saw him surrounded by angels who adored him and sang his praises. Sometimes when Our Lord thought of the souls who would not be saved — even by the most excruciating torments of his Passion — his agony in prayer brought sweats of blood. Mary was filled with sorrow and astonishment. Quoting Ven. Mary of Agreda: "Although the Evangelists, because they never intended to relate all the events of his life, mention this sweating of blood but once before his Passion, it is certain that this happened many times and in the presence of his most holy Mother; and this has been intimated to me several times."

When Mary had reached the age of thirty-three, which is the age of perfection in a human body, she was gifted in a way never equalled by another woman. Mary's beauty is described by the Franciscan mystic: "When therefore the Queen of heaven arrived at her thirty-third year, her virginal body had attained full natural growth, so well proportioned and beautiful, that she was the admiration not only of human beings, but of the angelic spirits themselves. She had grown in size and stature to the most perfect proportion in all the parts of her body and most strikingly resembled her divine Son in features and complexion when later on He arrived at that age; always, of course, taking into account, that Christ was the most perfect Man, while his Mother was the most perfect Woman."

At that age in others of our human race, corrupted nature begins to decline. The hair begins to whiten, the skin to wrinkle, some of the strength to weaken, and the whole human frame tends toward corruption. Even in her seventieth year, Mary still retained the same beauty and entirety that was hers at the age of thirty-three. Our Lord died at the age of thirty-three because his ardent love compelled him to bring the perfect gifts of nature and grace to the sacrifice of the Cross. We can also believe that the bodies of Adam and Eve were created as having reached this perfect age from the first moments of their existence.

Joseph too was growing older, and Mary noticed that

he no longer had the strength to continue his work so vigorously as he had done in younger days. Joseph's continual cares, journeys and labors for the sustenance of Jesus and Mary had weakened him more than his years. We are told that the Lord wanted to give him increased holiness in the virtue of patience and thus allowed him to feel sickness and pain.

Mary desired to show her gratitude for all he had done for Jesus and herself. She persuaded Joseph to discontinue his carpenter work, and allow her to take up the task of obtaining their necessities by her skill in spinning and weaving linen and wool. We quote the words of Ven. Mary of Agreda:"The Lord was not wanting in ability to provide for his bodily living, that of his blessed Mother and of Joseph. . . . He could have each day created the necessary food; but then the world would have been deprived of this spectacle of his holy Mother, Lady of the whole world, laboring for their sustenance; and the Virgin herself would have been deprived of the reward due to these meritorious works."

Having more leisure time now, Joseph was given joys of contemplation in the daily company of Jesus and Mary. He reached pinnacles of holiness not matched by other men. He had the best of nurses, his spouse Mary, to aid him in his sickness, giving him consolation and sustaining him with the greatest perfection and consideration. Mary procured what they could afford as the most healthful food for the nourishment of her husband, while she and her divine Son had the custom of eating fish, fruit, and herbs as their daily food.

The Lord was leading his Mother's most faithful spouse along the royal highway of the Cross. In the last years of his life, Joseph suffered various sicknesses such as fever, violent headaches, and painful rheumatisms, which greatly took away his failing strength.

Mary of Agreda tells us more: "In the midst of these

infirmities, he was suffering from another source, more sweet, but extremely painful, namely, from the fire of his ardent love which was so vehement, that the flights and ecstasies of his most pure soul would often have burst the bounds of his body if the Lord, who vouchsafed them, had not strengthened and comforted him against these agonies of love." Mary knew and understood all this, and was most joyful to labor for his support and comfort. She was aware of all this suffering and knew the occasions when he needed her most. Jesus also brought his divine comfort to this great man who had shared so deeply in the life of the Son of God.

Sometimes Mary would ask permission of Jesus, to use her power of prayer to stop the sufferings of Joseph and bring relief from his pains for a day or two. Other times, in answer to her pleas, angels appeared and spoke words in praise of the Divinity and its infinite perfections. Also the angels brought celestial joy in singing hymns of divine canticles to further inflame the love in the heart and soul of Joseph.

After eight years of enduring these sufferings, Joseph died as a soul most dear to our loving Creator. In the arms of Jesus, his natural life expired, and a lovely fragrance was noticed, even by persons walking near the house. Following the Jewish customs, his body was prepared for burial by Mary. As Ven. Mary writes: "Accompanied by the Redeemer of the world, his most blessed Mother and a great multitude of angels, and escorted by their friends and many others, the sacred body of the most glorious saint Joseph was borne to the common burying place. But on all these occasions and in these occupations, the prudent Queen preserved her composure and gravity, without allowing her countenance to exhibit any unwomanly or disorderly excitement; nor did her sorrow prevent her from attending to all that belonged to the service of her deceased spouse or her divine Son."

Joseph had been created with exceptional graces, making him worthy to be the spouse of the immaculate Queen and the putative father of the Redeemer of the world. In heaven, he has great powers of intercession for those who ask in a spirit of faith. Joseph died when he was sixty years old. He had become the husband of Mary at the age of thirty-three, and they had lived together for twenty-seven years. When Mary began her widowhood she had completed the half of her forty-second year.

Jesus promised Mary that he would remain with her in Nazareth until the time should come for him to begin his public life in obedience to his eternal Father.

Chapter 4

FOUR YEARS TOGETHER
AS MOTHER AND SON

Without Saint Joseph, there was a change in lifestyle at the little house in Nazareth. The Savior, now twenty-six years old, as the time for beginning his public life came nearer, began to show more openly the purpose of his life as the Redeemer of his people. As his helpmate, Mary grew in the knowledge of her Son as she cooperated in all that was revealed to her.

Mary of Agreda tells us: "The soul of Christ our Lord was a most transparent and flawless mirror, in which the blessed Mother saw reflected all the mysteries and sacraments which the Lord, as the Head and Artificer of the Holy Church, the Restorer of the human race, the Teacher of eternal salvation and the Angel of the great council, wrought and accomplished according to eternal decrees of the most blessed Trinity." Mary imitated and followed her divine Son as a perfect model in all he did.

It was the desire of Jesus that Mary now should find some relaxation from the many hours she had spent in attending to the needs of her deceased spouse through night and day. She was to join her divine Son in his prayers and noble works. Their needs were fewer, and it was not necessary for Mary to spend quite so much time in her weaving of wool and linen.

Of course, she always had the housekeeping tasks of cleaning and scrubbing, washing the dishes and cooking utensils, arranging the furniture, and keeping everything in order. Many times the angels assisted Mary in this work, even beginning it sometimes before she had the opportunity to do so. Because Mary had such a love for humility, she often tried to persuade the angels that such servile works were her duties, not for those who were already living in heaven.

When the angels provided heavenly music in their praises to Divinity, Mary often joined them, sometimes singing her own glorious hymns. We can imagine that her voice must have been extremely beautiful, just as everything else about her.

In these daily activities, Mary lost no moments in combining her actions with the constant awareness of Divinity in her ardent love and heavenly contemplation.

The food requirements of these two holy ones now consisted of one meal a day, usually taken in the evening about six o'clock. The menu was bread, herbs and fruit, sometimes fish also. Before this time they had accommodated themselves to the needs of Saint Joseph. When invited to eat with others, they gratefully accepted what was served in very moderate amounts.

The most tremendous sorrow for the incarnate Word and his faithful Mother was that so many souls would be refusing the graces of redemption. Mary's loving heart was torn asunder as she saw her beloved Son in his prayers shedding drops of blood in this agony. Mankind had been given freedom to accept or reject graces won at such a great expense. Mary could have died in the pains of her love without divine assistance.

The following words are quoted from our Franciscan mystic's writing: "In these great sorrows it sometimes happened, that the most loving Mother was overcome by deathly weaknesses, and they would no doubt have ended her life, if she had not been preserved by divine intervention. Her sweetest Son, in return for her most faithful and loving compassion, sometimes commanded the angels to console her and to sing her own heavenly canticles of praise in honor of the Divinity and humanity. At other times the Lord himself took her into his arms and gave her new celestial understanding of her exemption from this iniquitous law of sin and its effects. Sometimes, thus reclining in his arms, the angels sang to her in admiration, while she, transformed and enraptured in heavenly ecstasies, experienced new and exquisite influences of the Divinity."

In his infinite wisdom, Christ knew those who were predestined for various offices in the service of the future Church. Mary shared this knowledge. They understood the weaknesses in human nature: the denial of Peter; the unbelief of Thomas; the betrayal by Judas; and all the unwillingness of some unfortunate souls who would not accept the graces of redemption. They also had knowledge of all the blessed souls who would give their very lives for their boundless love of God.

Jesus was on fire with the burning desire to accomplish all of which divine power was capable for the salvation of souls. He could wait no longer to prepare the chosen people for his role as their living Messiah. In sorrowing love, he prayed and fasted, and began to spend time with the neighboring people, bestowing on them his hidden blessings. Sometimes he was away from Nazareth for two or three days, spending the nights in prayer on the mountains. While he was away the angels served Mary, letting her know all the actions of her divine Son. When he returned, sometimes having gone without rest, food or sleep, the loving Mother adored him and gave him all the comfort of her cooperating desires. In return for her gracious wishes to be of assistance to her Son and her fellowman, Jesus told Mary that the time had come, according to the will of his heavenly Father, that he should begin to prepare some souls to be able to accept his light and doctrine, and the knowledge that the Messiah was present in the world. Mary was asked to accompany him in all his excursions away from their town of Nazareth.

They went together to the surrounding areas and to some places in the province of Nephtali where Jesus performed miracles in a hidden way. He spoke to the people about the prophets and their testimonies already fulfilled, and that the Messiah was in the world. He reminded his listeners of the coming of the three kings and the slaying of the infants in Bethlehem. Many souls began to live a more virtuous life, inspired by this Teacher who was so graceful, peaceful and gentle. They were becoming ready to receive all that would happen when they would encounter him again in his public life. Sometimes Jesus and Mary spent the night in prayer under the starry sky. Angels accompanied them, protecting them from the inclemency of the weather and sometimes bringing them food.

Jesus consoled the sorrowful, relieved those who were oppressed, visited the sick, assisted those soon to die, cured some people of their illnesses, and helped those in great distress. Mary accompanied her divine Son as a faithful witness and co-worker, giving thanks for the blessings conferred on so many people. She imitated the works of her Son in her contacts with the women, while Jesus performed his works of mercy among the men.

Not all of these happenings escaped the notice of Satan. He saw that many sinners began to amend their lives and reject his evil tyranny. In the presence of Jesus or Mary, he felt a powerful force again hurling him and his demons into the flames of hell. He was filled with consternation and fury in this new defeat. If either Jesus or Mary had come to the sickroom, he had no power to assail a dying person with his wicked temptations.

Thus Mother and Son fulfilled the will of the heavenly Father in their four years together, bringing renewed hope to those who accepted their teachings.

Chapter 5

PREPARATION FOR A PUBLIC LIFE

> Now in those days John the Baptist came,
> preaching in the desert of Judea, and saying,
> "Repent, for the kingdom of heaven is at hand."
> For this is he who was spoken of through
> Isaiah the prophet, when he said, "The voice
> of one crying in the desert, 'Make ready the
> way of the Lord, make straight his paths.'"
> But John himself had a garment of camel's
> hair and a leathern girdle about his loins, and
> his food was locusts and wild honey. Then
> there went out to him Jerusalem, and all Judea,
> and all the region about the Jordan; and they
> were baptized by him in the Jordan, confess-
> ing their sins (Matt. 3:1-6).

Under the power of the Holy Spirit, at the age of thirty,
John began his public preaching in his role as Precursor
of our Savior. Mary had always provided for his necessities in the care of her angels. John had been sanctified
in the womb of his mother Elizabeth when Mary visited
her cousin before his birth, and he never lost that price-
less gift of holiness.

When Elizabeth received warning of the slaying of
infants in Bethlehem, under the cruelty of Herod, she had
fled with her son John to a place of safety in the desert.
When John was four years old Elizabeth died. He received
food every day from the angels sent by Mary until he
was seven years old. Then until he was nine years of age

he received only bread. After that it was the will of God
that his nourishment should be roots, wild honey and
locusts which he could obtain for himself. The angels
commissioned by Mary brought him consolation in his
solitude, and information about the activities and mysteries of the incarnate Word.

Ven. Mary writes: "His feet were bare, his features thin
and emaciated, his appearance wonderfully graceful, modest and humble, his soul was filled with invincible and
magnanimous courage, his heart inflamed with the love
of God and man, his words rang forth strong and force-
ful, piercing to the souls of his hearers like the sparks
from the immutable and divine essence of the Almighty.
He was gentle toward the meek, loving toward the humble, wonderful in the sight of angels and men, terrible to
the proud, dreadful to the sinners, and an object of horror to the demons." Graces from the Most High had made
John worthy and capable of his great task of Precursor
of Mary's divine Son.

The day arrived when Jesus should leave his mother in
Nazareth to continue in a more comprehensive way his
role as Redeemer of mankind. Mary had always known
this great sacrifice must take place when the time ordained
by the heavenly powers should be fulfilled. She was called
to a most exalted vision and heard the words: "Mary, my
Daughter and Spouse, offer to Me your onlybegotten Son
in sacrifice." Her motherly love for her Son was so deep
that it cannot be described in human words, excelling all
other loves in human hearts.

We can imagine in part the great sorrow in which Jesus
and Mary came to this hour of parting. It was imperative
that a time of prayer and fasting should prepare the Son
of God for the founding of his Church and his ensuing
Passion and Death. Mary would again have the graces to
know all that would be taking place in the soul of Jesus
until he would return to take her with him in the activi-

ties of his public life. As they walked to the door for this most sad of all farewells, Mary knelt for a blessing and kissed the feet of her Beloved.

> Then Jesus came from Galilee to John, at the Jordan, to be baptized by him. And John was for hindering him, and said, "It is I who ought to be baptized by you, and do you come to me?" But Jesus answered and said to him, "Let it be so now, for so it becomes us to fulfill all justice." Then he permitted him. And when Jesus had been baptized, he immediately came up from the water. And behold, the heavens were opened to him, and he saw the Spirit of God descending as a dove and coming upon him. And behold, a voice from the heavens said, "This is my beloved Son, in whom I am well pleased." (Matt. 3:13-17)

As Jesus walked alone on his way to the Jordan, he performed small miracles in a secret way. Among the people he encountered in different places, he relieved their necessities of body and soul. Before being baptized he gave no indications of his divine power in a public way.

During the absence of her divine Son, Mary remained in her house praying and imitating what she was shown in celestial visions concerning the prayers and actions of our Savior. At this time many angels were with her in a visible way, witnessing the sighs of her loving heart. With them she sang hymns of praise, glory, adoration and love to the Most High. She knew all that Christ would endure in his long time of fasting in the desert.

St. John had been given spiritual enlightenment informing him that Jesus the Redeemer was soon to be seen by him. After the ceremony of Baptism as told by St. Matthew took place, Jesus administered the sacrament to his Precursor John.

"This is my beloved Son, in whom I am well pleased." Ven. Mary of Agreda writes what was revealed to her: "Many of the bystanders heard this voice, namely, those who were not unworthy of such a wonderful favor; they also saw the Holy Spirit descending upon the Savior. This was the most convincing proof which could ever be given of the Divinity of the Savior, as well on the part of the Father, who acknowledged Him as his Son, as also in regard to the nature of the testimony given; for without any reserve was Christ manifested as the true God, equal to his eternal Father in substance and in perfection."

As a leader of his future followers, Christ went to a place in the desert where he would be in solitude, meriting graces of salvation for sinful mankind. In CITY OF GOD we read: "In satisfaction for our pride He offered his profound humility; for our avarice, his voluntary poverty and total privation of all that was his; for our base and lustful inclinations, his penance and austerity; for our hastiness and vengeful anger, his meekness and charity toward his enemies; for our negligence and laziness, his ceaseless labors; for our deceitfulness and our envy, his candid and upright sincerity and truthfulness and the sweetness of his loving intercourse." With all the enlightening graces and visions given to her, Mary continued to imitate the prayers and penances of Jesus in her solitude at Nazareth.

In Holy Scripture we read about the new defeat of Satan:

> Then Jesus was led into the desert by the Spirit, to be tempted by the devil. And after fasting forty days and forty nights, he was hungry. And the tempter came and said to him, "If you are the Son of God, command that these stones become loaves of bread." But

he answered and said, "It is written, 'Not by bread alone does man live, but by every word that comes forth from the mouth of God.'"

Then the devil took him into the holy city and set him on the pinnacle of the temple, and said to him, "If you are the Son of God, throw yourself down; for it is written, 'He will give his angels charge concerning you; and upon their hands they shall bear you up, lest you dash your foot against a stone.'" Jesus said to him, "It is written further, 'You shall not tempt the Lord your God.'"

Again, the devil took him to a very high mountain, and showed him all the kingdoms of the world and the glory of them. And he said to him, "All these things will I give you, if you will fall down and worship me." Then Jesus said to him, "Begone, Satan! for it is written, 'The Lord your God shall you worship and him only shall you serve." Then the devil left him; and behold, angels came and ministered to him (Matt. 4:1-11).

With the words of Jesus, Satan was forced to descend to the deepest caverns of hell with all the other evil spirits joining him. They were not given permission to roam the earth again until three days later. Angels came to serve our Lord with celestial food so that his holy body could be refreshed and invigorated again after his long fast. They also brought this celestial food to Mary at the command of Jesus. She had been most faithful in sharing her Son's prayer and penance. Satan was convinced that Jesus was a very, very holy man, but probably not the true Son of God.

Chapter 6

BEGINNING A PUBLIC LIFE
OF MIRACLES

In this chapter we shall endeavor to see the course of events as written in the Gospels and Mary's role as Mother of the Redeemer.

When our Lord left the desert after his forty days of prayer and solitude, he went again to the Jordan where John the Baptist pointed him out with the words: "Behold the Lamb of God." We read how some of the followers of the Baptist were then inspired to become followers of Jesus.

> Again the next day John was standing there, and two of his disciples. And looking upon Jesus as he walked by, he said, "Behold the Lamb of God!" And the two disciples heard him speak, and they followed Jesus. But Jesus turned round, and seeing them following him, said to them, "What is it you seek?" They said to him, "Rabbi (which interpreted means Master), where do you dwell?" He said to them, "Come and see." They came and saw where he was staying; and they stayed with him that day (John 1:35-39).

Divine enlightenment continued to come to Mary and all that Jesus did was made known to her. With the angels to guide her, Mary performed the same actions as her Son for the benefit of souls in Nazareth and the surrounding area. In a veiled way they taught the people that the Messiah was already in the world and explained what should be done for their salvation. Not only instructions were given but also hidden favors and private miracles were performed. Mary received new graces when she cooperated in the work of the Savior as commanded by the eternal Father.

Continuing words from the Gospel of St. John tell that Andrew was one of the two who had followed Jesus that day, and Ven. Mary writes that John was the other, though his name was not mentioned by the author of his Gospel in this passage.

Having spent this day with Jesus, Andrew knew that he had met the Messiah and told his brother Simon (Peter). The next day Philip and Nathaniel joined them and they departed for Galilee. However, Jesus did not go directly to Nazareth. They had much to learn before being introduced to Mary. The first five disciples selected to be in the company of Jesus were Andrew and Peter, John, Philip and Nathaniel.

> Now Andrew, the brother of Simon Peter, was one of the two who had heard John and had followed him. He found first his brother Simon and said to him, "We have found the Messiah (which interpreted is Christ)." And he led him to Jesus. But Jesus, looking upon him said, "You are Simon, the son of John; you shall be called Cephas (which interpreted is Peter)."

> The next day he was about to leave for Galilee, and he found Philip. And Jesus said to him, "Follow me." Now Philip was from Bethsaida, the town of Andrew and Peter. Philip found Nathanael, and said to him, "We have found him of whom Moses in the Law and the

Prophets wrote, Jesus the son of Joseph of
Nazareth" (John 1:40-45).

They went to various places in Galilee where Jesus
taught his heavenly doctrines and performed miracles (but
not in a public way). When his five first disciples were
sufficiently graced with faith in his divinity, Jesus
explained that Mary, his holy Mother, was a virgin in his
conception and remained a virgin during and after his
holy birth. With his teaching and cures of all maladies
Jesus was drawing them to the understanding of his nature,
human and divine. He also endowed them with admiration and reverence for Mary. When they reached Nazareth,
Mary was a most gracious hostess, and by her example
and words showed what great reverence should guide them
in their associations with her divine Son.

Mary of Agreda writes that Jesus administered the Sacrament of Baptism to Mary, and voices of the Trinity were
heard. The voice of the eternal Father: "This is my beloved
Daughter, in whom I take delight." The incarnate Word:
"This is my Mother, much beloved, whom I have chosen
and who will assist me in all my works." The Holy Spirit:
"This is my Spouse, chosen among thousands."

Saint John is the only Scripture writer who describes
in detail the happenings at Cana where Christ performed
his first public miracle. Mary had been invited to these
wedding celebrations of a relative of Saint Anne. Jesus
with his disciples also took part in the festivities. Jesus
and Mary reminded the bride and groom that now they
were entering a new state of life bound together in love
and faithfulness to one another. The fortunate couple were
blessed with all the graces necessary in this life-long com-
mitment.

Mary noticed that the supply of wine had run short.
She knew that Jesus would do something about it and
said to him, "They have no wine." And then to the atten-

dants, "Do whatever he tells you." Jesus told them to fill
the six water jars with water and take them to the chief
steward who was surprised to find the water jars contained wine which was richer than what had been served
previously. We read this in the beginning of John's chapter two.

> This first of his signs Jesus worked at Cana
> of Galilee; and he manifested his glory, and
> his disciples believed in him. After this he
> went down to Capharnaum, he and his mother,
> and his brethren, and his disciples. And they
> stayed there but a few days (John 2:11-12).

Many people began to believe in Jesus as the chosen
Messiah promised by God through the prophets. Twelve
were selected to be his closest companions as Apostles.

> Now it came to pass in those days, that he
> went out to the mountain to pray, and con-
> tinued all night in prayer to God. And when
> day broke, he summoned his disciples; and
> from these he chose twelve (whom he named
> apostles); Simon, whom he named Peter, and
> his brother Andrew; James and John; Philip
> and Bartholomew; Matthew and Thomas;
> James the son of Alpheus, and Simon called
> the Zealot; Jude the brother of James, and
> Judas Iscariot, who turned traitor (Luke 6:12-
> 16).

The chosen fishermen followed Jesus to
become "fishers of men".

Chapter 7

A PERFECT PARTNER FOR CHRIST

It was the desire of Jesus that his holy Mother should now begin to accompany him on his teaching journeys. From Cana they walked to Capharnaum, which at that time, was a large and highly populated city near the Sea of Tiberias. After a few days there, they proceeded to Jerusalem for the feast of the Pasch.

These journeys on foot in all sorts of weather were very fatiguing, especially for the Virgin Mary. Ven. Mary of Agreda writes: "What she endured in these labors alone is so great that not all the mortals together can ever satisfy their obligations to her in this regard. Sometimes by permission of the Lord, she suffered such great weakness and pains that he was constrained to relieve her miraculously. At other times he commanded her to rest herself at some stopping-place for a few days; while again on certain occasions, he gave such lightness to her body, that she could move about without difficulty as if on wings."

As we read in Holy Scripture, there were other women who accompanied Our Saviour.

> And it came to pass afterwards, that he was journeying through towns and villages, preaching and proclaiming the good news of the kingdom of God. And with him were the Twelve, and certain women who had been cured of evil spirits and infirmities: Mary, who is called the Magdalene, from whom seven devils had gone out, and Joanna, the wife of

> Chuza, Herod's steward, and Susanna, and
> many others, who used to provide for them
> out of their means (Luke 8:1-3).

Mary knew the whole doctrine of the evangelical law, but she always listened very reverently to the sermons of her Son. She continued to receive the grace to know the interior operations of the Soul of Christ, and joined her own prayers and supplications in union with his, asking that those who heard his words would receive them in a way which would secure their own salvation.

It was a great sorrow for Mary to know that some of the Redeemer's listeners would not accept the sanctifying graces which were presented by the incarnate Word. Quoting from CITY OF GOD again: "For the souls, that would not give entrance to divine grace and virtue, she sorrowed with ineffable grief, and was wont to shed tears of blood at the thought of their misfortune. What the great Queen suffered in this her solicitude and in her labors exceeds beyond all measure the pains endured by all the martyrs of the world."

Mary was also given the grace to know the interior dispositions of those who listened to the teachings of Jesus. In addition to her ceaseless fervent prayers, she instructed the women who traveled with her, and took care of their physical needs as well as their more important treasures. Not only in her sweet conversations, but also in her actions, she taught them the practice of charity by visiting the sick in the infirmaries, the poor, and prisoners. She also performed the duties of a nurse to the wounded, consoled the sorrowful, and gave aid to others in need.

Our Lady did not forget about the needs of the men following in the company of the Savior — especially the chosen Apostles. When they had any doubts, this holy lady was very prudent in explaining whatever was necessary for their understanding. "They were enlightened by her wisdom, chastened by her humility, quieted by her modesty, enriched by all the blessings that flowed from this storehouse of all the gifts of the Holy Spirit." She lived her role as Mother and Queen, serving them all with the privilege of obtaining the help of the angels whenever she asked for their assistance.

Ven. Mary writes: "According to what has been given to me to understand, it is certain that she brought about not only many miraculous conversions, but she cured the blind and the sick, and called the dead to life." These miracles were performed by Mary, but done with such great secrecy that all the glory would go to our Redeemer.

Ven. Mary also tells us: "She contented herself with the assistance she could render by private instruction and conversation, which she did with celestial wisdom and efficacy. By this assistance and by her prayers, she secured more conversions than all the preachers of the world."

Satan saw all that was happening as men and women listened to the words of Jesus and began to be converted from their sinful ways. The demon was confused because he was losing his power and wondered if the Messiah was now truly in the world. He also saw the wonders performed by John the Baptist, influencing many to lead a more holy way of life. Both resisted his wicked temptations. If one of them was the divine Word, which could it be? We quote from Mary of Agreda: "Both," (he said to himself) "are great Saints and Prophets; the life of the One is that of the common people, but yet extraordinary and strange in some respects; the other performs many miracles and his doctrine is nearly the same. Both cannot be the Messiah; but let Them be whoever they may, I recognize Them as my great Enemies and as Saints, and must persecute Them until I have undone Them."

When Herod had John put in prison an awaited opportunity came for the demon to use Herodias and her dancing daughter as instruments to achieve his evil plan. If

John had called himself a Voice, perhaps that was his way of disguising the meaning of divine Word. In Holy Scripture we read what happened on the day of Herod's birthday banquet and his promise to give what might be requested by the daughter of his adulterous partner.

> And the king said to the girl, "Ask of me what you wish and I will give it to you." . . . Then she went out and said to her mother, "What am I to ask for?" And she said, "The head of John the Baptist." And she came in at once with haste to the king, and asked, saying, "I want you right away to give me on a dish the head of John the Baptist."

> And grieved as he was, the king, because of his oath and his guests, was unwilling to displease her. But sending an executioner, he commanded that his head be brought on a dish. Then he beheaded him in the prison, and brought his head on a dish, and gave it to the girl, and the girl gave it to her mother. His disciples, hearing of it, came and took away his body and laid it in a tomb (Mark 6:22-29).

Through divine power, and in celestial light, Jesus and Mary had come to the prison where John was awaiting his death. They were visible only to John, and unknown to the executioners. This heavenly visit of Jesus and his Mother was a wonderful preparation for a martyr's death with the promise of a glorious future awaiting the faithful Precursor of the true Messiah.

Another quote from CITY OF GOD: "As soon as the Precursor beheld before him the Redeemer and his Mother in the midst of the angelic host, his chains fell from him and his wounds were healed. With ineffible joy he prostrated himself on the ground and in deepest humility and admiration asked the blessing of the incarnate Word and his Blessed Mother."

What God desires, most of all, to teach us about our Queen is her constant humility. Ven. Mary of Agreda devotes an entire chapter to telling how Mary lived this virtue in the most holy way. A paragraph in that chapter is quoted: "There was in Mary an excellence of humility altogether singular and peculiar to her; for neither the full knowledge that she was the Mother of God, nor the consideration of all the wonders that she wrought, or that were wrought by her divine Son, nor her position as the Keeper and Dispenser of all the divine treasures, as the most immaculate among all creatures and as the most powerful and most favored of all God's creatures, could ever cause her heart to forsake the place she had chosen in estimating herself as the lowest of all the handiwork of the Most High. O Rare humility!"

Chapter 8

A TRUE SPIRITUAL MOTHER FOR THE FOLLOWERS OF CHRIST

Mary of Agreda tells that Our Lord's favors to the Apostles depended in a great part on their devotion and love toward his holy Mother, and her special love toward them. Those coming to the forefront are Peter who would lead the first members of the Church; John the most beloved of all, and James the brother of John. These three were the ones chosen to be present with Jesus in the scene of his Transfiguration, and closest to him in the garden of his Agony. Two other persons mentioned in this chapter are the ardent lover Mary Magdalene and the avaricious Judas who sold his soul to the devil.

As John became the favorite of Jesus, this loving relationship was also extended to Mary. This Apostle tried to please Our Lady in every way he could. His thoughtfulness was always rewarded by the heavenly Queen. We read a brief description of John: "The Evangelist besides chastity and virginal purity, possessed some other virtues which were especially pleasing to the Queen; among them were a dovelike simplicity, as is manifest from his writings, and a great gentleness and humility, which made him most meek and tractable. The heavenly Mother always looked upon the peaceful and the humble as the most faithful imitators of her divine Son. On this account the blessed Queen favored John above all the other Apostles. . . . From the very first moment of his vocation John commenced to excel all the rest in piety toward the Mother Mary and to fulfill the least of her wishes as her most humble slave."

Judas also received special attention from Mary. In the beginning of his Apostleship he had favorable intentions of becoming a diligent follower of Christ. However, he became very proud and began to notice the faults of the other eleven. He made unfavorable judgments, not recognizing those same frailties in himself. Their company became irksome to him and many times he absented himself from the group. When it became necessary for someone to be in charge of the donations and necessary expenditures, Judas immediately wanted this position. He fell into the situation described by St. Paul:

"What the Apostle says in his first letter to Timothy was literally fulfilled in this treacherous disciple: 'For they that will become rich, fall into temptation and into the snares of the devil and into many unprofitable and hurtful desires, which drown men into destruction and perdition. For the desire of money is the root of all evils; which some coveting have erred from the faith and have entangled themselves in many sorrows'" (1 Tim. 6,9).

Mary knew this and tried to encourage Judas to amend his ways which, if continued, would lead him to disaster. She began to show more consideration for him in a special way. When Judas asked that she use her influence with Jesus she replied: "Consider well, my dear, what you ask, and examine whether your intentions are upright. Ponder well, whether it is good for you to seek that which all your brethren fear and refuse to accept, unless they shall be compelled thereto by the command of their Lord and Master. He loves you more than you love yourself and without doubt knows what will benefit you; resign yourself to his most holy will, change your purpose, and seek to grow rich in humility and poverty. Rise from your fall, for I will extend you a helpful hand and my Son will show you his loving mercy." All her efforts and entreaties were rejected by the unhappy Apostle.

With daring presumption Judas made his request to

Jesus himself. Our Lord spoke these words: "Do You know, Judas, what you seek and what you ask? Be not so cruel toward your own self as to solicit and seek to obtain the poison and the arms which may cause your death."

Judas, as the greatest of hypocrites, made this reply: "Master, I desire to serve you by employing my strength in the service of your faithful followers and in this way I can do it better than in any other; for I offer to fulfill all the duties of this office without fail."

Judas was warned of the danger in which he was placing himself, but he was too avaricious to heed these words of advice. In Scripture we find his words of complaint about the extravagance of Mary Magdalene and the words of Christ to defend her. Judas would not have given the money to the poor as alms, but would have used it for his own interests.

In CITY OF GOD we read these words about Mary Magdalene: "Magdalene also had a share in her special love; for Mary knew that the love of this woman for her Son was most ardent and that this great penitent was eminently chosen for the manifestation of the magnificence of God's mercy toward men. Most holy Mary distinguished her before the other women in her familiar intercourse and enlightened her in regard to most exalted mysteries, by which she inflamed still more the love of Magdalene toward Jesus and toward herself. The holy penitent consulted the heavenly Lady in regard to her desire of retreating into solitude in order to live in continual contemplation and penance; and the sweetest Mother instructed her in the deep mysteries of solitary life. This life she afterwards embraced with the consent and blessing of the Queen."

Among the early followers of Jesus, the two most beloved were John and Mary Magdalene standing beneath the Cross of Jesus with our holy Queen.

Chapter 9

OUTPOURING OF DIVINE LOVE

> Tell the whole community of Israel: On the
> tenth of this month every one of your fami-
> lies must prepare for itself a lamb, one apiece
> for each household (Exodus 12,3).

As the days drew nearer to the great celebration of the
Pasch, Jesus and Mary, the Apostles and other disciples
began their journey from Galilee to Jerusalem. Jesus was
full of loving desires in knowing that the time for his
Passion and Death to redeem the human race would soon
take place. His prayer began in this manner: "My eternal
Father, in compliance with your holy will I gladly hasten
to satisfy your justice by suffering even unto death. Thus
shall I reconcile to you all the children of Adam, paying
their debts and opening to them the gates of heaven which
have been closed against them. I shall seek those who
turned away and lost themselves, so that they may be
restored by the force of my love."

Mary again shared in all ways possible her perfect union
with the divine Word. She knew his thoughts and echoed
them in her own heart and soul as coadjutrix. A part of
her prayer is quoted: "O would it were possible, that I
receive the pains and sorrows which await him, and that
I might suffer death in order to save his life! Accept,
heavenly Father, the sacrifice of my sorrowing affection,
which I offer in union with him in order that your holy
will and pleasure may be fulfilled." The sufferings of
Mary exceeded beyond our comprehension those of all

the martyrs in the world taken together until the end of time.

In the Gospels we read about Our Lord's triumphal entry into Jerusalem as foretold by the prophet. Mary did not accompany Jesus on this day because she wanted all the glory to be given to her Son alone.

> Rejoice heartily, O daughter of Sion, shout for joy, O daughter Jerusalem! See, your king shall come to you; a just savior is he, meek and riding on an ass, on a colt, the foal of an ass (Zach. 9,9).

The Pharisees and Scribes were infuriated when seeing the homage given to Jesus the true Messiah and tried to find an excuse for putting him to death. Perhaps it was a welcome surprise for their wickedness when Judas came with his plan to betray his Master for thirty pieces of silver. Jesus and his Mother were aware of all this, and Mary tried once more to admonish Judas sweetly, trying to dissuade him in his wicked scheme; but being entirely in the power of the demons, he would not listen to her pleas.

During the days which followed, Jesus continued his teaching in the Temple at Jerusalem. In the evenings he returned to Bethany where he had raised Lazarus from the dead.

Thursday evening was the time appointed for eating the Passover meal, the eve of the Passion and Death of our Savior. At early dawn Jesus spoke these words to Mary: "My Mother, the hour decreed by the eternal wisdom of my Father for accomplishing the salvation and restoration of the human race and imposed upon Me by his most holy and acceptable will, has now arrived; it is proper that now we subject to Him our own will, as we have so often offered to do. Give Me your permission to enter upon my suffering and death, and as my true Mother, con-

sent that I deliver Myself over to my enemies in obedience to my eternal Father. In this manner do you also
willingly cooperate with Me in this work of eternal salvation, since I have received from you in your virginal
womb the form of a suffering and mortal man in which
I am to redeem the world and satisfy the divine justice.
Just as you, of your own free will, did consent to my
Incarnation, so I now desire of you to give consent also
to my Passion and Death of the Cross. To sacrifice Me
now of your own free will to the decree of my eternal
Father, this shall be the return which I ask of you for having made you my Mother; for He has sent Me in order
that by the sufferings of my flesh, I might recover the
lost sheep of his house, the children of Adam." Mary of
Agreda writes: ". . . no created tongue can describe the
tender and mournful affections of that purest of hearts
and the sighs of her inmost soul. She was as the mysterious turtledove, that already began to feel the approach
of that solitude, which the company of no creature in
heaven or on earth could ever relieve or compensate."

In the Gospels of the four Evangelists, especially in
that of St. John, we read accounts of the Last Supper —
the time of Christ's outpouring of divine love. From CITY
OF GOD we learn several elaborations not found in Holy
Scripture. We are told that Jesus had sent Peter and John
into the city to make arrangements for the eating of the
Passover meal as prescribed in the Law of Moses. The
house chosen was that of a very gracious and wealthy
disciple. It contained a large hall perfectly furnished for
the occasion and an adjoining room which would enable
Mary to see all that would transpire on this holy night.
As early evening approached, Jesus and his Apostles arrived
in Jerusalem and Mary with her holy companions soon
followed. They observed all the customs in the ways prescribed.

When the ceremonial Passover meal had been completed, Jesus girded himself with a large towel and began to wash the feet of the Apostles, beginning with Peter. In the Gospel of St. John we read about Peter's reaction.

Judas was still among the number, and Jesus washed his feet with greater tenderness than the other eleven, thus showing pardon and love if he would accept it. Ven. Mary writes: "The outward aspect of Christ our Lord was most exquisitely charming and attractive; his countenance, serenely dignified, yet sweetly expressive and beautiful, was framed in abundant waves of golden chestnut hair, freely growing after the manner of the Nazarenes; his frank and open eyes beamed forth grace and majesty; his mouth, nose and all the features of his face exhibited the most perfect proportion and his whole Person was clothed in such entrancing loveliness, that He drew upon himself the loving veneration of all who beheld Him without malice in their hearts. Over and above all this, the mere sight of Him caused in the beholders an interior joy and enlightenment, engendering heavenly thoughts and sentiments in the soul." Judas knew this loving Savior was at his feet. But the heart of this unfortunate Apostle had become so hardened that he would not even look upon the face of his Master and God. He rejected all the grace that would have been his salvation.

Jesus prayed to the Father:

> While I was with them, I kept them in your name. Those whom you have given me I guarded and not one of them perished except the son of perdition in order that the Scripture might be fulfilled (John 17,12).

At the beginning of her Holy Eucharist revelations, Ven. Mary writes: "With great diffidence do I enter upon the treatment of this ineffable mystery of the Holy Eucharist and of what happened at its institution; for, raising the eyes of my soul toward the light which encompasses and governs me in the performance of this work, the high intelligence given me of these vast wonders and sacraments reproaches me with my littleness in comparison with the greatness therein manifested."

The ceremonial meal and washing of the feet having been completed, Jesus ordered that the low table around which they had reclined while eating, should be removed, and a higher table brought to take its place. This was to be the altar for the institution of the Sacrament of Holy Eucharist. A very rich cloth covered the table. Then a costly plate and a cup like a large chalice were placed thereon. These seemed to be made of a precious stone like emerald, and sometimes were later used by the Apostles for certain occasions. At the request of Christ, unleavened bread and wine were brought.

"Then the Master of life spoke words of most endearing love to his Apostles, and, though his sayings were wont to penetrate the inmost heart at all times, yet on this occasion they were like the flames of a great fire of charity, which consumed the souls of his hearers." Jesus instructed them more deeply than before in the mysteries of his divinity, humanity and works of the Redemption.

These revelations impressed each one according to his own disposition and the role to be played by him in salvation history. John was still the most beloved of the Apostles as new enlightenments were given to him. We can realize this in reading his Gospel account of the Last Supper. Mary saw and heard all this and as before, through divine power, she cooperated as Mother of the Church.

Raising his eyes to heaven, Jesus spoke the words of consecration, changing the bread into his true Body; then immediately said the words of consecration to change the wine into his true Blood. He held up these two parts of the Sacrament for the adoration of all those present, including the angels who had come from heaven. Mary, with her power given by Divinity, had commanded the demons to descend to their abodes in hell while the institution and reception of this holy Sacrament took place.

Satan and his demon companions had been allowed to be present at the ceremonial supper and washing of the feet. They also would witness the entire Passion of Christ to be sure that Jesus was the true Messiah and Redeemer, God and man.

After the consecration Jesus received his own Body and Blood, offering Himself in this blessed Sacrament as a sacrifice for our salvation. Jesus then took another particle of the consecrated Bread and gave it to the archangel Gabriel who communicated it to his holy Mother as her first Holy Communion.

We quote again: "The most blessed Sacrament was deposited in the breast and above the heart of the most holy Virgin Mother, as in the most legitimate shrine and tabernacle of the Most High." The sacred host remained there until after the Resurrection when St. Peter gave Mary the Holy Eucharist again in his first Mass. "The sacramental species were not consumed or altered in the heart of the Lady and Queen of heaven until the next consecration."

The sacramental bread and wine were then distributed to the Apostles, who were commanded to divide it among themselves and partake of it. "By this commandment Jesus conferred upon them the sacerdotal dignity and they began to exercise it by giving Communion each to himself. This they did with the greatest reverence, shedding copious tears and adoring the Body and Blood of our Lord, whom they were receiving." Thus they were given the power of the priesthood as founders of the holy Church.

Judas remained with the other Apostles at this time, and had thoughts of how he might desecrate the sacred species and present it to the priests for the further condemnation of Jesus. Our Lady was given the power to know the interior dispositions of the ones who received the holy Sacrament. She also knew the wicked plot of Judas. Seeing that he would be next to receive in the seating arrangement, Mary used her power of command, telling the angels to remove the Holy Eucharist from Judas, purify it from contact with him, and restore it to its original place. This was done without the notice of the other eleven. Perhaps this can teach us more about the nobility of Jesus, shielding the honor of his most wicked Apostle to the very end.

Chapter 10

COADJUTRIX OF THE REDEEMER

The truths revealed in this section of Mary of Agreda's revelations present a new and unknown secret of Our Lady's total love. According to her desires, she was given the miraculous grace to actually feel in her own body every pain being inflicted on the body of Christ. This was done by divine decree in an unbloody manner, showing no visible evidence of the wounds she was sharing with our Redeemer. Without miraculous divine assistance, she could have died many times over.

> And they came to a country place called Gethsemane and he said to his disciples, "Sit down here, while I pray." And he took with him Peter and James and John, and he began to feel dread and to be exceedingly troubled. And he said to them, "My soul is sad, even unto death. Wait here and watch" (Mark 14:32-34).

When her divine Son was leaving the hall of the Last Supper, Mary met him and adored him as her God and Redeemer. Mary of Agreda writes: "At this face to face meeting of the Prince of eternity and of the Queen, a sword of sorrow pierced the heart of Son and Mother, inflicting a pang of grief beyond all human and angelic thought." With a Son's true love, Jesus said: "My Mother, I shall be with you in tribulation; let us accomplish the will of the eternal Father and the salvation of men."

Jesus with his Apostles proceeded to Mount Olivet,

while Judas slipped away to where the Jewish leaders were assembled. By a special favor of divine grace, Mary was able to see and hear all the activities of her divine Son. She followed him in a perfect imitation of all that happened in the garden of Gethsemane. When Jesus chose Peter, John and James to be with him in a place beyond where the other eight Apostles were urged to pray, Mary selected the three most fervent in her group of holy women to retire with her to another room to watch and pray.

Mary of Agreda writes: "According to our way of understanding, there was a contention or altercation between the most sacred humanity and the Divinity of Christ. For this humanity, in its intense love for men who were of his own nature, desired that all should attain eternal salvation through his Passion; while his Divinity, in its secret and high judgments, had fixed the number of the predestined and its divine equity could not concede its blessings to those who so much despised them, and who, of their own free will, made themselves unworthy of eternal life by repelling the kind intentions of Him who procured and offered it to them. From this conflict arose the agony of Christ, in which he prayed so long and in which he appealed so earnestly to the power and majesty of his omnipotent and eternal Father."

When Jesus was perspiring blood in his agony, Mary also did. When the archangel Michael came to Christ, the archangel Gabriel came to Mary. When the moment for the capture of our Savior arrived, Mary made it known to her companions who shared her sorrows in most bitter and abundant tears; especially overcome with grief was the one known as Mary Magdalene.

Judas had arrived with a large band of soldiers and servants of the high priests and Pharisees, all equipped with their lanterns, swords, clubs, and whatever else was necessary for their capture of Jesus.

When Our Lord said, "I am He" divine power made all

his enemies with their dogs and horses fall to the ground. Lucifer and his demons also were deprived of motion with new confusion. They remained this way for seven or eight minutes until, through the intercession of Mary, they were given divine permission to rise.

Mary saw in her visions each of the Apostles as they fled from the garden in fright. She prayed for each of them in their deep distress while Lucifer influenced them with new temptations against their faith and trust in their divine Master. Peter and John, being more fervent than the others, later were courageous enough to follow their captured Lord at a distance to the court of the high priest Caiphas.

After the betrayal kiss, the men sent by the Jewish leaders bound Jesus in a most painful way. They wound a heavy iron chain around his waist and neck. The two ends which remained free were attached to large rings or handcuffs for our Lord's hands to fasten them behind his back. They also used two pieces of strong rope, putting one around the throat of Jesus and crossing it at the breast with heavy knots all about the body. Two long ends were left in front. The second rope was used to tie his arms, bound likewise around his waist, leaving the two long ends behind. They did all this with insulting blows and vilest language. Then they left the garden in tumult and uproar, pulling on the ropes sometimes in front, sometimes in back, causing our Savior to fall many times. In this way his divine face was wounded and lacerated. While he was on the ground, they added blows and kicks, trampling upon his body. Lucifer and his demons urged them on to even more cruelty.

In CITY OF GOD we read, "When the servants of the high priest laid hands on and bound the Savior, the most blessed Mother felt on her own hands the pains caused by the ropes and chains as if she herself was being bound and fettered; in the same manner she felt in her body the blows and torments further inflicted upon the Lord, for, I have already said, this favor was granted to his Mother, as we shall see in the course of the Passion. Thus her sensible participation in his sufferings was some kind of relief of the pain, which she would have suffered in her loving soul at the thought of not being with Him in his torments."

Mary also knew the fate of Judas and wept bitterly for this traitorous Apostle. Two sentences are quoted: "In this one act of treason he committed so many and such formidable sins, that it is impossible to fathom their immensity; for he was treacherous, murderous, sacrilegious, ungrateful, inhuman, disobedient, false, lying, impious and unequalled in hypocrisy; and all this was included in one and the same crime perpetrated against the person of God made man." His conscience made him realize what he had done. He was filled with remorse and rage against himself. "Gnawing like a wild beast at the flesh of his arms and hands, striking fearful blows at his head, tearing out his hair and raving in his talk, he rushed away and showered maledictions and execrations upon himself as the most unfortunate and miserable of men." Mary of Agreda writes more telling how he hanged himself and how the demons carried him to hell.

Jesus was then dragged through the streets first to the house of Annas, then to that of Caiphas where he was accused of blasphemy and deserving of death. Ven. Mary writes this about his captors, "Roused by satanic fury they all fell upon their most meek Master and discharged upon Him their wrath. Some of them struck Him in the face, others kicked Him, others tore out his hair, others spat upon his venerable countenance, others slapped or struck Him in the neck, which was a treatment reserved among the Jews only for the most abject and vile of criminals."

When it was already past midnight, the highpriest and his supporters decided to have our Lord taken to the dungeon and carefully guarded so that he could not escape. Then the captors dragged Jesus to the prison cell most filthy and unfit for any human being. They continued their torture by binding Christ to a short pillar in a very painful stooping position. The one chosen to guard Jesus followed the suggestions of the demons and invited his wicked comrades to come in and torture Christ again in ways prompted by the forces of evil.

"While they were discussing this matter, a multitude of angels, who assisted the Redeemer in his Passion, when they saw Him so painfully bound in such an improper and polluted place, prostrated themselves before Him, adoring Him as their true God and Master, and showing Him so much the more reverence and worship the more they admired the love which moved Him to subject Himself to such abuse for the sake of mankind. They sang to Him some of the hymns and canticles which his own Mother had composed in his praise."

Our Lady's words confided to our Spanish mystic: "Great was the sorrow, most bitter the grief, of my most holy Son, that not all should make use of the fruits of his Redemption. This same thought also pierced my heart and immensely added to the sorrow of seeing Him spit upon, buffeted, and blasphemed more cruelly than can ever be understood by living man."

"But next to this sorrow, my greatest one was to know, that after all these death-dealing sufferings of the Lord, so many men should still damn themselves even within sight of all the infinite treasures of grace."

When Friday morning dawned, the council composed of ancients, chief priests and scribes met to make the decision that Jesus should be brought before Pontius Pilate for the death sentence.

Mary was just beginning to leave the Canacle with her holy companions when the Apostle John arrived. He asked forgiveness for his failure to remain with Jesus when he was betrayed in the garden and Mary asked him to accompany her while the angels made a pathway through the crowd. At a sharp turn of the street they met Jesus. "Mother and Son looked upon each other with ineffable tenderness, interiorly conversing with each other in transports of an unspeakable sorrow." Jesus was then led to the Roman Procurator while Mary followed.

Pilate knew that Jesus was innocent and that the Jews had delivered up their Messiah out of envy and malice. This Roman Procurator was in a very difficult position, and learning that Jesus was a Galilean, he ordered that our Savior be taken to Herod for judgment. Herod, the Governor of Galilee at that time, treated Christ as an enchanter and conjurer, even allowing his servants to clothe Jesus in a white tunic, the garment of a fool. Our Savior maintained complete silence in the presence of Herod. Again our Lord was taken to the palace of Pilate. Mary met her divine Son as the crowd left Herod's hall of judgment.

We quote again: "The sight of the white vestment, by which they proclaimed Him fit to be treated only as an insane fool, pierced Mary's heart with new sorrow; though She alone of all mankind, recognized the mystery of his purity and innocence indicated by this vestment. She adored Him in it with deepest reverence and followed Him through the streets back to the house of Pilate."

Ven. Mary tells this about the scourging allowed by Pilate who thought this punishment would influence the Jews to release our Master. The scourging was administered by six men who were filled with the fury of Satan, the number of lashes being 5,115 — and let us remember that our Lady felt all the pains in her own body in the same intensity as they were felt by Christ.

The first two men struck our Lord with hard and thick cords full of rough knots; the second pair with hardened leather thongs; the third pair with extremely rough rawhides dried hard like osier twigs. Then came the crowning with thorns, more painful than we can imagine.

We read these words about Mary: "Although she shed no blood except what flowed from her eyes with her tears, nor was lacerated in her flesh; yet the bodily pains so changed and disfigured her, that John and the holy women failed to find in her any resemblance of herself."

We see our "Queen of virtues" remaining unconquered even though being overwhelmed in grief beyond any human thought. In all her actions she was most prudent, courageous and admirable, shedding constant tears with the dignity of a queen.

The death sentence was read in a loud voice before all the people and the heavy cross was placed on the wounded shoulder of Jesus. The great multitude of people, with the executioners and soldiers, began to move through the streets with great uproar and confusion to Mount Calvary.

On reaching the place of crucifixion, every further torture possible was inflicted on our Savior as he was nailed to the cross for our redemption. It was the custom in a crucifixion to give the victim a drink of strong and aromatic wine to help him bear his torments. To Jesus they gave a drink mixed with gall to torment his sense of taste. When preparing the bar of the cross for the nailing of the hands of Jesus, they made the holes farther apart than necessary so that his bones would be wrenched from their sockets when the nails would pierce his hands. The executioners roughly removed the tunic of Jesus to which some of his wounds which had dried were opened again; the crown of thorns was pulled off with the tunic and with greater cruelty it was placed on again, opening new wounds in his adorable head. With more cruelty the cross bearing the adorable body of our Savior was fastened in the hole prepared for it, and Jesus suffered for three more hours in excruciating agony. Mary alone understood all the mysteries of his dying words:

"Father, forgive them, for they know not what they do!" (Luke 23:34)

"Amen I say to thee, this day thou shalt be with Me in Paradise." (Luke 23:43)

"Woman, behold thy son." "Behold thy mother." (John 19:26,27)

"My God, My God, why hast Thou forsaken me?" (Matt. 27:46)

"I thirst." (John 19:28)

"It is consummated." (John 19:30)

"Father, into thy hands I commend my spirit." (Luke 23:46)

When Mary saw a band of soldiers approaching Calvary, she wondered what further acts of cruelty would be done to the dead body of our Savior. In order to hasten the death of the two crucified criminals, the soldiers were to break their legs. Seeing that Jesus was already dead, they did not break his bones, but the centurion called Longinus thrust his spear into the Sacred Heart of Jesus. This lance thrust was felt by Mary, and she said, "The Almighty look upon you kindly with eyes of mercy for the pain you have caused to my soul."

Some of the blood and water flowing from the side of Christ fell on the face of Longinus and restored his eyesight which had been almost lost. With the divine light entering his soul, he was instantly converted and proclaimed boldly that Christ was the true Son of God.

Soon another group of men approached, and John assured Mary that they were friends. Mary had experienced another source of anxiety — how to provide a proper burial for the holy body of Jesus. In answer to her prayers, two influential disciples, Joseph and Nikodemus, came with servants carrying all that would be necessary for removing the sacred body from the cross. Joseph provided the burying cloths and the new tomb in which the Lord of heaven could be placed. Nikodemus brought about a hundred pounds of myrrh and aloes to be used in the customs of the Jews for the burial of distinguished men.

They tenderly removed the crown of thorns and reverently handed it to Mary. She kissed it reverently and pressed it to her face. Then the nails were removed and handed to Mary for her veneration and that of the other persons who shared her sorrow. Then the sacred body was placed in the arms of our Sorrowful Mother. The day was getting late and all the burial necessities had to be completed before sundown.

The sacred body was then embalmed, using all the aromatic ointments and spices which Nikodemus had provided. Our Lord's body was then placed on a bier to be carried by John, Joseph, Nikodemus, and the centurion Longinus to the sepulcher. At Mary's request choirs of angels came in shapes, visible only to her, to form a procession. They were followed by the blessed Mother, Mary Magdalene, and the other disciples who had been inspired to come to Calvary after the lance-thrust. All were in silence and tears as the sacred body of Christ was placed in the tomb. After acts of adoration, the stone was rolled to the entrance of the grave.

The darkness of night had fallen when Mary and her companions returned to the Cenacle. Mary was most admirable in her consideration of others, asking John to provide her holy friends with any refreshments or other items which might be needed. She herself retired to be alone.

Mary must have remembered those first words from the infant Jesus: "Become like Me, my Beloved." How faithfully she had done just that!

Chapter 11

A REWARD IN GLORY

Ven. Mary of Agreda tells that the divine soul of Christ stayed in Limbo from half past three of Friday afternoon until after three on Sunday morning when it was joined to the sacred body in the tomb.

At that same moment Mary was "transformed from sorrow to joy, from pain to delight, from grief to ineffable jubilation and rest"—all in exquisite glorious beauty. The risen Christ came to Mary, filling her with glorious love proportionate to the sufferings she had experienced in his Passion. Jesus gave her all the glory that could be given to a creature so pure and altogether so pleasing to the Trinity.

During the forty days before his Ascension, when our Savior was not making his appearances to others, he remained in the Cenacle with his beloved Mother.

The owner of the house where the Last Supper had been celebrated invited Mary to stay there while she was in Jerusalem. This was called the Cenacle and became a meeting place for the Apostles and the early followers of Jesus.

Mary was given the graces to be aware of all that happened in the manifestations of her Son to his special friends chosen for this privilege. These persons came to her in great joy to tell their stories while she listened in thoughtful delight.

Another miraculous favor was the enjoyment of seeing and speaking with the spirits of her parents and her spouse Joseph amid the company of angels. Together they sang hymns and canticles in praise of God — many of them composed by Mary herself.

One day when Mary was at prayer, the Blessed Trinity appeared upon a throne and Mary was invited to join them. Each of the three Persons spoke special words to her. The Father said: "My Daughter, to you do I entrust the Church founded by my Onlybegotten, the new law of grace He established in the world, and the people, which He redeemed; to you do I consign them all." The Holy Spirit, "My Spouse, chosen from all creatures, I communicate to you my wisdom and grace together with which shall be deposited in your heart the mysteries, the works and teachings and all that the incarnate Word has accomplished in the world." The Son said, "My most beloved Mother, I go to my Father and in my stead I shall leave you and I charge you with the care of my Church; to you do I commend its children and my brethren, as the Father has consigned them to Me."

In the last chapter of the revelations written by our Spanish mystic in Volume III, there is a secret unknown to many. When the day came for Jesus to ascend to his heavenly glory from the highest point of Mount Olivet, one hundred and twenty persons were chosen to be witnesses. Among them were his Mother, the eleven Apostles, the seventy-two disciples, Mary Magdalene, Lazarus and the other faithful men and women who were true followers of Christ. We have recorded many of the spiritual experiences of Mary. In this chapter we find a miracle even more exalted than the others. Mary was taken up to heaven with her glorious Son amid choirs of angels. She was given a place at the right side of Jesus on his throne. The disciples left on earth saw only Jesus rising upward through the skies.

The holy Trinity regaled her with new delights and gave her a choice to remain there or to return to earth where she would be of assistance to those still in pilgrimage in the primitive Church.

While Mary was in heaven for three days, she also remained with the other persons on earth. If more than one saint has had this spiritual grace of bilocation, how can we doubt that this is true for the heavenly Queen who is so holy and perfect? Again we quote: ". . . the divine power enabled the blessed Mother miraculously to be in two places at once, remaining with the children of the Church for their comfort during their stay in the Cenacle and at the same time ascending with the Redeemer of the world to his heavenly throne, where she remained for three days. There she enjoyed the perfect use of all her powers and faculties, whereas she was more restricted in the use of them during that time in the Cenacle."

We end this section of writing with a quotation from the words spoken by Mary to those who would read: "It seemed to me a sacred duty, that I deprive myself of the eternal felicity of which I was in possession and, returning from heaven to earth, gain new fruits of labor and love for the Almighty; all this I owed to the divine Goodness, which had raised me up from the dust."

Last paragraph of Volume III:

"Let it all be for the glory and honor of the Most High, the King of the ages, the Immortal and Invisible (Tim. 1,27), and for that of his Mother, the most blessed Mary, through all the eternities!"

THE CORONATION

The heavenly Life of the Queen of Heaven, most holy Mary, containing the Events of her Life from the Coming of the Holy Spirit until the Assumption and Coronation of the Virgin Mother of God in Heaven.

INTRODUCTION

In the beginning of Volume IV, holy Mary of Agreda has written a long introduction, telling of her hesitation in beginning to write these most marvelous treasures of Mary's heavenly life. Many words of divine encouragement were given to her. We quote words from the Lord and words from our Lady.

Our Lord, "Remember, soul, that you cannot continue what you have begun, nor will you finish the writings of my Mother's life, if you will not become altogether perfect and pleasing in my eyes. For I wish that you gather within you the copious fruits of this benefit, and that you among the first, profit by it in greatest abundance. In order that you may share its fruits as I wish, it is necessary, that all which is earthly in you and savoring of a daughter of Adam be consumed. You must be free from the effects of sin with all its evil inclinations and habits."

Our Lady, "My daughter, understand well, that these desires, which the Most High again excites in your heart, are pledges and effects of his love, by which He calls you to his intimate intercourse and familiarity. It is his most holy will and mine, that you on your part correspond to them in order that you may not hinder your vocation or retard any longer the pleasure of his Majesty in what He requires of you. It is time you raise yourself to a perfect imitation of Me, clothing yourself with new strength and extending your hand to strong doings. By such a life and behavior you will be able to begin what still remains to be written; for it must be written in such a way, that you put in practice the lessons it inculcates. Without such a disposition you will not be able to write it; since it is the will of the Lord, that my history shall be written more in your heart than on paper, and that you feel what you write, in order that you may write what you feel."

As a servant of the Queen of the Angels, I find a meaning meant for me also. Religious life is different now from what it was in a seventeenth century Spanish cloister. God has arranged for me, in this twenty-first century, a situation of freedom in many ways, although I feel a definite need for the guidance of obedience and humility. Mary is so wonderful that her love and influence can still be known and practiced in a fervent modern life with the God who says, "Be holy because I am holy."

In order to do my part in revealing a new look at the glories of Mary, I feel a true need for the intercession of the beloved Apostle John, who alone knew the mysteries of Mary in a way in which no other person has ever been favored. With him I place all my trust in the hearts of Jesus and Mary.

THE CORONATION

CONTENTS

Chapter 1

WAITING FOR THE POWER OF THE PARACLETE

The beloved Apostle John, in a vision, saw Mary ascend with Christ to heaven and later return to earth in dazzling glorious beauty.

> And I saw the holy city, the new Jerusalem, coming down out of heaven from God, prepared as a bride adorned for her husband (Rev. 21:2).

Only this short passage of John's book of Revelation is quoted here. In Volume I of Mary of Agreda's CITY OF GOD and in this abridgment writing of that same volume, a reader can find how this and other passages of John's writing are an interpretation of the glories given to our powerful immaculate Queen. It was necessary for John to use such enigmatic language because there was a danger that the early Christians could fall into idolatry, worshiping Mary as a god.

Scripture in the Old Testament tells that the face of Moses, after speaking with God was so overwhelmingly brilliant that the Israelites could not look at him unless he covered his face with a veil. Mary's heavenly radiance caused a similar effect until her glorious beauty had moderated. We read this about St. John: "Two days he remained as it were entranced and suspended in admiration at this extraordinary mystery. Knowing that his most holy Mother had descended from on high, he desired to speak to her, but dared not presume."

On the third day he persuaded himself to enter her presence. The effect it had when he saw her caused him to fall prostrate to the floor, not being able to rise until Mary herself enabled him to do so.

Among the first words Mary spoke to him were these: "My Master and son, you already know that I am to be governed in all my actions by obedience to you; for you take the place of my divine Son and Master, in order to command me in all that I am to do. I now ask you anew to be solicitous in commanding me, on account of the consolation I derive from obeying in all things."

John felt confused and perplexed because of what he had seen about her glory. He wanted to be her slave, but at last had to yield to the request of this Queen of humility.

Ven. Mary writes: "The vision of the great Queen of the angels in her state of glory was so deeply impressed upon the understanding and the interior faculties of the Evangelist, that the image of it remained within him during all his life. At the moment when he saw her descend from heaven, he cried out in great wonder. The intelligence he then received concerning her he afterwards manifested in his writing of Revelation, especially in the twelfth and twenty first chapters."

In paragraph 33 we again find words worth quoting.

"In order that She might enlighten His Church in the first ages, her Son sent Her and made Her known to the first children of his holy Church. In the course of ages He has continued to manifest her holiness and greatness by the wonders performed by this Queen and by innumerable favors and blessings flowing from her hands upon mankind. In these last ages, which are the present, He will spread her glory and make Her known in new splendor, on account of the Church's great need of her intercession and of her help against the world, the demon and the flesh. For these, through men's own fault, as we see even in our day, will assume greater sway and strength to hinder the working of grace in men and to make them more unworthy of glory. Against this new malice of Lucifer and his followers, the Lord wishes to oppose the merits and intercession of purest Mary and the light sent into this world by the example of her life. She is to be the refuge and sanctuary of sinners and the straight and secure way, full of splendor for all that wish to walk upon it."

Ven. Mary writes: "I again remind those who shall read this history not to be astonished at the hidden sacraments recorded of the most blessed Mary therein, nor to hold them unworthy of belief, because they have not been until now revealed to the world. For, even setting aside the fact that they are all worthy and befitting this great Queen, we cannot deny, that, though we have until now no written record of her wonderful doings after the Ascension of the Lord, yet we must suppose Her to have wrought many and exceeding great wonders in her office as Teacher, Protectress and Mother of the new evangelical Church, which was to be introduced into the world under her assistance and supervision."

After the visible effects of her heavenly splendor had gradually diminished, the glorious Mother began, in sweet conversation, to bring to the minds of her Cenacle companions, the teachings and instructions given them by the divine Savior. There were about one hundred twenty persons in the group. In prayer and fasting, they were to prepare for the coming of the Holy Spirit as promised by Jesus.

This was done under the care and direction of beautiful Mary. Each day they followed a schedule as follows: As the Teacher for the first Christians, the heavenly Lady spoke in the form of a conference, explaining with deeper meaning the divine mysteries; a time of discussion followed; then a time of vocal prayer in reciting the Our Father and some of the Psalms, with the remaining time in mental prayer. In the early evening they ate a meal of bread and fish before retiring for a moderate amount of sleep.

On one of these days Mary experienced a surprising visit from her divine Son. This was the first time, but not the last. Jesus remained with her for several hours in rewarding consolation and delight. Of course, this was far beyond our human limitations.

Mary knew beforehand all that would happen according to God's holy will. Our heavenly Queen asked her angels to inspire the minds and hearts of the Apostles, especially Peter and John, to request her aid so that she could obey them in their office and dignity as priests of the Most High.

It was decided that another disciple should be chosen to take the place of the traitor Judas, again bringing their number to twelve as it had been.

> And they put forward two: Joseph, called Barsabbas, who was surnamed Justus, and Matthias. And they prayed and said, "Thou Lord, who know the hearts of all, show which of these two you have chosen to take the place in this ministry and apostleship from which Judas fell away to go to his own place." And they drew lots between them, and the lot fell upon Matthias; and he was numbered with the eleven Apostles (Acts 1:23-26).

It was fitting that this should be done according to the directions of Saint Peter in beginning his chosen role as Christ's Vicar on earth and head of the pilgrim Church. All were united in this selection of Matthias as the twelfth Apostle.

They remained in prayer awaiting to receive what had been promised - the mystery of the great Paraclete!

Chapter 2

THE FIRST PENTECOST
WITH MARY

Mary knew the hour in which the Holy Spirit would come. In her extraordinary graces she was shown the Father and the Son determining how the Holy Spirit would accomplish all that would be plentiful for the knowledge of others. We read this about the desires of the Word. "He besought his Father also, that, besides bringing grace and the invisible gifts, the Holy Spirit appear in the world in visible form, that so the evangelical law might be honored before all the world; that the Apostles and faithful, who were to spread the divine truth, might be encouraged, and that the enemies of the Lord, who had in this life persecuted and despised Him unto the death of the Cross, might be filled with terror." We are told that all this would happen at the third hour (nine o'clock) as the chosen ones were gathered in prayer with our heavenly Queen.

"The air resounded with a tremendous thunder and the blowing of a violent wind mixed with the brightness of fire or lightning, all centering upon the house of the Cenacle. The house was enveloped in light and the divine fire was poured out over all of that holy gathering. Over the head of each of the hundred and twenty persons appeared a tongue of that same fire, in which the Holy Spirit had come, filling each one with divine influences and heavenly gifts and causing at one and the same time the most diverse and contrary effects in the Cenacle and in the whole of Jerusalem, according to the diversity of the persons affected."

"In the most holy Mary these effects were altogether divine, and most wonderful in the sight of all the heavenly courtiers; for as regard us men, we are incapable of understanding and explaining them. The purest Lady was transformed and exalted in God; for she saw intuitively and clearly the Holy Spirit, and for a short time enjoyed the beatific vision of the Divinity. Of his gifts and divine influences She by Herself received more than all the rest of the saints."

The Apostles were confirmed in grace, never to be lost. The new gifts of Wisdom, Understanding, Knowledge, Counsel, Piety, Fortitude and Fear of the Lord were theirs in abundance. These graces enabled them to accomplish all miracles necessary in their great task as founders of the new Church, especially Peter as the first Vicar of Christ, and John as the son and protector of the Queen of the Angels.

Those outside the Cenacle saw the miraculous light and heard the tremendous thunder and wind, not knowing the cause until they heard Peter's words. Those who had shown compassion in seeing the terrible sufferings of Jesus were converted and became ardent followers of Jesus. Others who had shared in actively causing his Passion received terrible chastisements.

"By the dreadful thunders and violent commotion of the atmosphere and the lightnings accompanying his advent, He disturbed and terrified the enemies of the Lord in that city, each one according to his own malice and perfidy. This chastisement was particularly evident in those who had actively concurred in procuring the death of Christ, and who had signalized themselves in their rabid fury against Him. All these fell to the ground on their faces and remained thus for three hours. Those that had scourged the Lord were suddenly choked in their own blood which shot forth from their veins in punishment for shedding that of the Master. The audacious servant, who had buffeted the Lord, not only suddenly died, but was hurled into hell body and soul. Others of the Jews, although they did not die, were chastised with intense pains and abominable sicknesses . . . This chastisement became notorious in Jerusalem, although the priests and Pharisees diligently sought to cover it up, just as they had tried to conceal the Resurrection of the Saviour."

The demons in hell also felt these terrors, being deprived of their power and remaining that way for three days. Of course, their fury made them inflict new torments on the souls who also occupied a place in their abode.

In the Acts of the Apostles we read:

> Now there were staying at Jerusalem devout Jews from every nation under heaven. And when this sound was heard, the multitude gathered and were bewildered in mind, because each heard them speaking in his own language. But they were all amazed and marvelled, saying, "Behold, are not all these that are speaking Galileans? And how have we heard each his own language in which he was born? Parthians and Medes and Elamites, and inhabitants of Mesopotamia, Judea, and Cappadocia, Pontus and Asia, Phrygia and Pamphylia, Egypt and the parts of Libya about Cyrene, and visitors from Rome, Jews also and proselytes, Cretans and Arabians, we have heard them speaking in our languages of the wonderful works of God" (Acts 2:5-11).

Peter and the other Apostles left the Cenacle to speak to the crowds gathered around the house; many converts, as told in Scripture, were enlightened and asked to receive Baptism. The holy women who had been in the Cenacle group also received the graces to perform miracles.

Our Queen remained in fervent prayer, knowing all that was taking place in Jerusalem.

Chapter 3

LIVING IN A TIME OF MIRACLES

As saint Peter spoke to the listening crowd his Spirit-filled words touched the hearts of many, exciting within them feelings of sorrow and contrition. "Let the whole house of Israel understand, and let them be assured, that God has made this Jesus, whom you have crucified, his Anointed and the Lord of all, and that He has raised Him from the dead on the third day."

In answer to their questions concerning repentance and salvation, Peter's words again brought the desired effect. "Do penance and be baptized every one of you in the name of Jesus Christ for the remission of sins; and you shall receive the gift of the Holy Spirit. For the promise is to you, and to your children, and to all that are far off, whomsoever the Lord shall call. Seek therefore now to make use of the remedy, and to save yourselves from this perverse and incredulous generation."

The remaining hours of the day were spent in a harmony among the men and women who had been in the group of disciples in the Cenacle. The holy women attended to their needs, just as they had done while Jesus was still with them. The Sacrament of Baptism was administered by the Apostles to those who had been prepared for it by the assistance of the other disciples.

In the evening some of the new converts met our Blessed Mother. Again Peter's words told them more.

"My brethren, and servants of the Most High, this is the Mother of our Redeemer and Master, Jesus Christ, whose faith you have received in acknowledging Him as

186

true God and man. She has given Him the human form, conceiving Him in her womb, and she bore Him, remaining a virgin before, during and after his birth. Receive Her as your Mother, as your Refuge and Intercessor, for through Her you and we shall receive light, direction, and release from our sins and miseries." Mary, who knew the sentiments of each individual, listened with the kindness of a true mother.

Ven. Mary writes this about the favors granted through the presence and intercession of our Queen: "For she did not rest or lose one moment or occasion of conferring some favor either upon the whole Church or some of its members. For she consumed Herself either in praying and beseeching her divine Son, without ever experiencing a refusal, or in exhorting, instructing, counseling, and, as Treasurer and Dispenser of the divine favors, distributing graces in diverse manners among the children of the Gospel. Among the hidden mysteries, which were made known to me concerning this power of the blessed Mary, was also this, that in those first ages, during which she lived in the holy Church, the number of the damned was proportionately very small; and that, comparatively, in those few years a greater number were saved than in many succeeding ages."

These first Christians formed a joyful community, sharing their resources among one another for the benefit of the poor. Some of the recent converts brought their exquisite jewelry to Mary. She received them with true gratitude, but kept nothing for herself. Through the hands of saint John and others appointed for the task, they were used in a way to help the less fortunate among them. Those with wealth put their money into a common fund. It is rather startling to read in Scripture that Ananias and his wife Sapphira fell dead at the feet of saint Peter when they had kept a part of their money for themselves.

The first Mass to be celebrated in this new Christian

Church was offered on the octave of Pentecost. Peter, in his office as the Vicar of Christ, was to be the celebrant. Under Mary's direction the hall of the Last Supper was arranged just as it had been when Our Lord was visibly among them. With the aid of Mary's angels and the holy women, everything was made immaculately clean. The same vessels that had been used by our Savior were set upon the altar. Mary prepared the bread and wine to be used at the Consecration and Holy Communion.

Some of us have wondered if the consecrated bread, which we believe is truly the body of Christ, may contain a part of Mary's substance also. Our Lady has given these words to Ven. Mary of Agreda: "Observe also that which you have added yourself in order to do reverence to the sacramental flesh and blood as coming from my womb and as having been nourished and grown from my milk. Ever keep up this devotion; for the truth you have perceived, that the consecrated body contains part of my own blood and substance, is in fact real."

With great reverence, the Apostles, the closest followers of Jesus, and the newly baptized persons prepared for the reception of Holy Communion, each praying in his or her own heart with deep feelings of humility, unworthiness and love. Then were recited the same psalms and prayers used by Christ. We continue quoted sentences. "Saint Peter took in his hands the unleavened bread, and, after raising up his eyes to heaven with admirable devotion, he pronounced over the bread the words of consecration of the most holy body of Christ, as had been done before by the Lord Jesus." Visible angels filled the Cenacle with a splendor of light, shining especially over our heavenly Queen. "Then saint Peter consecrated the chalice and performed all the ceremonies, which Christ had observed with the consecrated body and blood, raising them up for the adoration of the faithful." Holy Communion was received in both forms by Peter, the Apostles, our Lady Mary, and the closest followers of Jesus. The newly baptized received only the form of bread.

The new sacred host after being received by our Lady remained in her heart as had happened when she received Holy Communion at the Last Supper.

"This favor began at the first Communion and through the preservation of the species continued until the second Communion received at the hands of saint Peter on the octave of Pentecost. Then, as the new species took their place in her heart, the former ones were consumed. By this miraculous exchange, the previous sacramental species continued to yield their place to those she received in her Communions until the end of her life, so that she was never deprived of the presence of her Son and God in sacramental form."

The Mass was concluded with the recitation of some psalms and prayers offered in thanksgiving by saint Peter and the other Apostles. "Our great Queen and Lady gave thanks to the Most High for all of them, and the Lord was pleased with her thanksgiving, granting the petitions which his Beloved offered up for the present and the absent in his holy Church."

Some of Mary's words to our Spanish mystic in this part of her writing: "Without penance there shall be no grace, without reform no pardon, without pardon, no glory. But just as these are not conceded to those that are unworthy, so they are also never denied to those that are worthy; nor is ever the mercy of God withheld from anyone who seeks to obtain it."

Chapter 4

THE QUEEN'S POWERS OF PROTECTION AND GUIDANCE

To see such love and holiness in these first Christians infuriated the enemy Satan, who had been completely conquered on Calvary. When allowed by the Most High to again roam the earth, he and his fellow demons looked for ways to lead the followers of Christ into sin, and to give up their fervor in many ways through human weaknesses. Mary knew all his wicked procedures and frustrated his plans.

Part of her prayer to God is quoted: "Let me, eternal Lord, fight the battles against your enemies. Clothe me with your power in order that I may humiliate them and crush their pride and haughtiness."

Satan and his followers decided to work through the Jewish leaders to begin a persecution of the Apostles and their Christian companions.

Peter and John miraculously healed a paralytic. This was a miracle publicly acknowledged for the man was well known in the city, and the unbelieving Jews arrested the two Apostles who were commanded to do no more preaching in the name of Jesus the Nazarene. Our Lady knew all that was happening and again used her power to cast the devils back to the depths of hell.

Mary of Agreda tells this: "The infernal dragon could not resist the mandate of the powerful Queen; for her divine Son, to the greater terror of the demons, permitted them all to see Him sacramentally present in the bosom of the invincible Mother, as in the throne of his omnipotence and majesty."

When some of the Apostles went to neighboring towns, and no longer remained with Mary for a few days, Satan tried to ensnare them with his wicked temptations, but Mary's angels always defeated the companions of Satan.

As the number of the faithful continued to grow, so did the graces of heavenly protection increase in our Queen. With her own hands she took special care of the poor, the infirm, and the dying in their spiritual needs and physical necessities. One example is given here.

A certain young woman of poor parentage became very ill and was in danger of dying and losing her immortal soul. Lucifer saw her condition, and used all his powers to make her begin to draw away from Mary and the other disciples. He showed himself as another woman and told her she was wrong in believing the truths taught by the Apostles. One of the faithful disciples who usually visited the sick, heard of her approaching death and went to see her. But she had been so deceived by the devil that she would not even listen to his words of comfort and encouragement. He then went to saint John to tell him about her serious condition. The Apostle went to the sick girl immediately, and spoke to her words of eternal life if she would only listen, but she had been so influenced by the deceptions of Lucifer, that John also could do nothing to help her. He hurried to Mary, asking for her help.

Mary prayed very fervently for help from God. She sent one of her angels to defend this dying one against the powerful demons, but even an angel could not overcome the girl's obstinacy in clinging to her false illusions. When the angel returned to Mary, he told her of all his efforts but could not succeed in changing the mind of the dying young woman. Our Lady planned to walk the long distance to the girl's dwelling, but angels immediately assisted her, carrying her in a cloud to the sick-room to find many devils ready to snatch the poor girl to hell.

"As soon as the Queen of Angels made her appearance all the evil spirits vanished like lightning and as of falling over each other in their dismay. The powerful Queen commanded them to descend into hell and remain there until she should permit them to come forth, and this they were forced to do without the least power of resistance."

Mary remained with the young woman for two hours before she was called to eternal life. Mary of Agreda writes this:

"Her assistance was so effectual that she not only brought the young woman to the path of eternal life, but delivered her soul from all guilt and punishment. She sent her immediately to heaven accompanied by some of the twelve angels that bore on their breasts the sign of the Redemption and palms and crowns in their hands as special guardians of the devotees of the great Queen."

We read this about the Mother of God:

"This wonder was wrought by the wisdom of God, in order that the angels, the saints of heaven, the Apostles and also the demons might know the resistless power of most holy Mary and in order that they might learn that, as she was the Mistress of all, so not all of them together could equal her in power; that nothing would ever be denied to her prayers in favor of those who loved her, served her or called upon her."

One of the most fervent and fearless of the followers of Jesus was a young man named Stephen who merited a special love and care from Mary. He was gifted with heavenly wisdom, fortitude, and intrepid, dauntless courage. Because he was steadfast in his disputes with the Jewish leaders, accusing them of crucifying their promised Messiah, he incurred their deepest hatred. Many times his enemies tried to kill him, but he was warned by our Queen of the times and places where his Jewish foes were waiting to secretly seize him.

Ven. Mary tells this: "The blessed saint corresponded in most faithful attention and deepest reverence with the benefits conferred upon him by Christ our Savior and his heavenly Mother; for he was not only of a peaceful, but of a humble heart, and those that are so disposed in truth, are thankful for all benefits, even though they may not be so great as those conferred on saint Stephen."

Mary, who had knowledge of his future martyrdom, spoke these words to him: "You Stephen, shall be the first-born of the martyrs, engendered by my divine Son and Lord by the example of his death; you shall follow his footsteps, like a privileged disciple his master, and like a courageous soldier his captain; and at the head of the army of martyrs, you shall carry his banner of the Cross. Hence it is meet that you arm yourself with fortitude under the shield of faith, and be assured, that the strength of the Most High shall be with you in the conflict."

This knowledge increased his invincible faith, and even more the love in his devoted heart.

When the time did come for his martyrdom, as we are told in the Acts of the Apostles, he was led before the Jewish leaders in their court of judgment. He took the opportunity to prove that Jesus was truly the Messiah who had been promised through all the prophets of the Old Testament, and had been rejected by his chosen people. In their deep anger, the priests accused him of blasphemy, and led him out to the place of stoning. Mary knew all that was happening and prayed that her Son would arrange for her to be with saint Stephen in his last hour.

Angels carried their Queen in splendor and glory to the place where this was happening and Stephen's face shone with heavenly light at the sight of Mary. Through her intercession his martyrdom was filled with wondrous glory.

Mary then returned to her Cenacle oratory, leaving

Stephen in the care of her angels, while she continued her prayers of powerful intercession.

". . . the heavens opened and the Savior appeared to him standing at the right hand of the Father in the act of assisting him in the conflict. Saint Stephen raised his eyes and said, 'Behold I see the heavens opened and its glory, and in it I see Jesus at the right hand of God himself.' " As the cruel process of stoning continued, our martyr said, "Lord, receive my Spirit." Then, on his knees in a loud voice, "Lord, lay not this sin to their charge."

More words are quoted from CITY OF GOD: "In these prayers he was supported by those of the blessed Mary, who was filled with incredible joy to see the faithful disciple imitating so closely his divine Master by praying for his enemies and persecutors and commending his spirit into the hands of his Creator and Redeemer."

Ven. Mary ends this chapter with the words: "I have dilated upon his history, because I have been shown the great holiness of this first martyr, and because he was such a devout and highly favored disciple of the most holy Mary."

Chapter 5

MARY'S SOLICITUDE FOR
THE JOURNEYING APOSTLES

After the death of St. Stephen, the unbelieving Jews were inspired by Lucifer and his demons to begin a fearful persecution of the newly founded Church in Jerusalem. Many of the new Christians left the city with the blessings of the Mother of Jesus who remained there with the Apostles. Mary spent many hours in prayer to know and follow the desires of the Most High.

We quote again from Ven. Mary's writing: "In all her thoughts, she was most exalted; in wisdom she was beyond comparison; in counsel, most prudent; in her decisions most equitable and clear-sighted; in her works, most holy; in her words, true and sincere; in all goodness, lovable. Toward the weak, she was most kind; toward the humble, sweet and loving; toward the proud, reserved and majestic. Neither did her own excellence inflate her, nor adversity disturb her, nor labors cast her down; in all her activities she was a faithful copy of her divine Son."

Our Queen knew the time would soon come for the Apostles to begin their missionary journeys to other parts of the world. She began a special time in prayer and fasting for forty days. Before the forty days were completed, she called the Apostles together for the writing of the one set of truths to be professed by all the members of the Christian faith wherever thy might be. This is what we know today as the Apostles' Creed. In preparation for this, Peter and the other eleven met for the last ten days of

195

Mary's time of prayer and fasting to receive the true inspirations of the Holy Spirit.

On the last day of prayer, Peter celebrated Mass. While they continued in prayer, the sound of thunder was heard and the Cenacle was filled with brilliant light. The Apostles began to speak the inspired words:

1. Saint Peter: I believe in God, the Father almighty, Creator of heaven and earth.

2. Saint Andrew: And in Jesus Christ, his only Son, our Lord.

3 and 4. Saint James the Greater: Who was conceived through operation of the Holy Spirit, born of the Virgin Mary.

5. Saint John: Suffered under Pontius Pilate, was crucified, died and was buried.

6 and 7. Saint Thomas: Descended into hell, arose from the dead on the third day.

8. Saint James the Less: Ascended into heaven, is seated at the right hand of God the Father Almighty.

9. Saint Philip: From thence He shall come to judge the living and the dead.

10. Saint Bartholomew: I believe in the Holy Spirit.

11. Saint Matthew: In the holy Catholic Church, the Communion of saints.

12. Saint Simon: Forgiveness of sins.

13. Saint Thaddeus: The resurrection of the flesh.

14. Saint Matthias: Life everlasting. Amen.

With the help of angels, copies were soon made and distributed to the Christians living in other places at that time. It carried miraculous happenings to some of the areas where the faithful were gathered.

After a full year had passed, the Apostles knew it was time to leave Jerusalem and go to other countries, teaching the truths proclaimed by their Savior. With the advice of Mary, they prayed and fasted for ten days to be filled with the power of the Most High. At the conclusion of this time of prayer, Mass was celebrated by Peter and again in a visible way with majestic light; miraculous graces were bestowed on them through the action of the Holy Spirit.

United in their thoughts, they said in unison a prayer of which part is quoted: "We wish to be spared no labors, difficulties or tribulations in the performance of this work, even unto death. But distrusting our weakness, we beseech You, Lord God most High, send upon us your divine Spirit to govern and direct our footsteps in the imitation of our Master and to visit us with his strength. Manifest and instruct us to which kingdoms and provinces each of us shall depart according to your good pleasure for the preaching of your holy Name."

A divine voice was heard, saying these words: "My vicar Peter shall point out the province, which falls to each one. I shall govern and direct him by my light and spirit." Peter then began with himself, saying: "I, my Lord, offer myself to suffer and die in imitation of my Lord and Redeemer, preaching the faith at present in Jerusalem, and afterwards in Pontus, Galatia, Bythinia and Cappadocia, provinces of Asia; and I shall take up my residence at first in Antioch and afterwards in Rome, where I will establish my seat and found the Cathedra of Christ our Redeemer and Master, and where the head of his Church shall have his residence." He continued with the assignments, dividing among them the countries of the world which were known at that time. Only one of the eleven is being quoted here:

"Our most dear brother John shall obey the will of our Savior and Master as made known to him from the Cross, discharging the duties of a son toward our great Mother and Mistress. He shall serve Her and assist Her with filial reverence and fidelity; he shall administer to Her the sacred mysteries of the Eucharist and shall also take care of the faithful in Jerusalem during our absence. And when our God and Redeemer shall have taken into heaven his most blessed Mother, he shall follow his Master in the preaching of the faith in Asia Minor, governing the churches there established from the island of Patmos, whither he shall retire on account of persecution."

At the conclusion of the assignments, a loud thunder was heard and more light came upon them with the words: "Let each one accept his allotment."

They prostrated themselves upon the ground and said together: "Most High Lord, thy word and the word of thy vicar we obey with a prompt and joyous heart, and our souls rejoice and are filled with thy sweetness in the abundance of thy wonderful works."

The Apostles received an abundance of new knowledge and power, including an understanding of the cultures and people to whom they were sent, the ability to understand and to be understood in the many foreign languages which they would encounter, and the power of performing miracles. Sometimes they would be transported by angels to different places as we read in Scripture about St. Philip. At times this was necessary when any of them needed to consult Peter or their Mistress Mary. The spiritual gifts conferred on the Apostles were extraordinary in all ways that would be an advantage for them as chosen to be the voice of Christ to the nations.

We are told that Mary received higher graces than all of them. She was given an understanding of the spiritual states of those who would be their converts and all the difficulties which these twelve men would experience.

When the days of their departures came, Mary gave them garments like those which her divine Son had worn, being similar in color and texture. Her angels had assisted her in making them. She also gave each a small metal case in which she had placed three of the thorns which had pierced the head of Jesus, and pieces of cloth which she had used to wipe away the most precious blood of Christ in his Circumcision and Passion.

We quote again: "All these miracles and innumerable others unknown to us, were necessary to these men, who were to be sent to so many kingdoms, provinces, and peoples yet in possession of the devil, full of idolatries, errors and abominations, which were the condition of the world at the time the incarnate Word came to save the human race."

Chapter 6

A MIRACULOUS CONVERSION

Through the great visions and infused gifts which holy Mary had received, she was altogether perfect in being the Guide, the supreme Mistress, Mother, Governess and Sovereign of the Church, which was now placed in her hands. She is the true and faithful Dispensatrix of all graces so needed by mankind for an eternal joy in a heaven as planned by our loving Creator.

Mary of Agreda continues her writing with a chapter about the glorious Saint Paul. His character is revealed in these words: "Saul was of a disposition generous, magnanimous, most noble, kind, active, courageous and constant . . . a staunch professor of the law of Moses, being studious and learned in it, having a retentive memory and keen understanding." Saul was convinced that it was right to oppose the new way of life taught by Jesus.

It was revealed to our Queen that this zealous person called Saul was destined to become a Champion of the Christian faith to the Gentiles. He would be changed in a miraculous conversion from an instrument of Satan to an instrument of Christ.

Satan was infuriated to see how the group of people following the teachings of Jesus and Mary was continuing to grow in numbers. After the death of St. Stephen, another persecution of the early Christians was begun by Satan and his demons acting through human individuals. Saul seemed to be the one best qualified to carry out their wicked plans.

"In his impious presumption Lucifer tried to induce

Saul to attempt single-handed the life of all the Apostles, and with still greater presumption, even the life of the most blessed Mary. To such a point of insanity rose the pride of this most bloodthirsty dragon. But he deceived himself. The disposition of Saul was most noble and generous, and therefore it appeared to him beneath his dignity and honor to stoop to such crimes and act the part of an assassin when he could, as it seemed to him, destroy the law of Christ by the power of reasoning and open justice. He felt a still greater horror at the thought of killing the most blessed Mother, on account of the regard due to her as a woman; and because he had seen her so composed and constant in the labors and in the Passion of Christ." However, Saul did obtain permission from the chief priests to search for the Christians in Damascus and bring them as prisoners to Jerusalem.

By her fervent prayers, Mary hastened the time of Saul's marvelous conversion. A part of her prayer is quoted: "Do not then my Son and Lord, despise the prayers of your Mother; let your divine decrees be executed and let me see your name magnified; for the time and occasion are opportune and my heart cannot suffer such a blessing to be delayed."

Mary's prayers to her Son were irresistible. Jesus descended from heaven to be with her in person. He could not make any further delays in the conversion of Saul. His words are quoted: "My Mother, chosen among all creatures, let your will be done without delay. I will do with Saul as you ask, and will change him, that from this moment he will be a defender of the Church which he persecutes, and a preacher of my name and glory. I shall now proceed to receive him immediately into my friendship and grace."

"Shortly afterward the Lord appeared to Saul on the road near Damascus. . . . The Lord showed himself to Saul in a resplendent cloud amid immense glory, and at

the same time Saul was flooded with divine light without and within, and his heart and senses were overwhelmed
beyond power of resistence." He fell from his horse and
heard the divine words, "Saul, Saul, why do you persecute Me?"

"Who are you, Lord?"
"I am Jesus whom you persecute; it is hard for you to
kick against the goad of my omnipotence."
"Lord, what do you command and desire to do with
me?"
"Arise and go into the city, and you will be told what
to do."

Saul's companions heard the words, but did not see the
heavenly light which had overwhelmed their leader. They
led him into Damascus where he remained in prayer and
fasting for three days until the word of God led Ananias
to cure his blindness and receive him into the Church.

Many divine secrets were revealed to Saul, making
him a new person with the name Paul. Mary of Agreda
writes: "Thus it happened that in the same short time,
in which Lucifer through pride was changed from an
angel to a devil, the power of Christ changed Saul from
a demon into an angel in grace. In the angelic nature
the highest beauty turned into the deepest ugliness; and
in the human nature the greatest perversity into the highest moral perfection."

Paul's complete dedication for the remainder of his life,
saw him ardently devoting his whole being to the pro-
claiming of the Gospel truths established by the Son of
God. He also was given the grace to know that this salvation was obtained through the intercession of Mary our
Queen. How he desired to see her and let her know how
sorry he was for his past actions in persecuting the followers of her Son. Mary knew the sentiments of his heart,

and sent an angel with messages of comfort and encouragement. The angel then returned to our Lady with the grateful message which Paul wished to convey.

Mary of Agreda tells us, "Greater is this wonder than the creation of heaven and earth with all the creatures; greater than to give sight to the blind, health to the sick, life to the dead. Let us congratulate the sinners on the hope inspired by this wonderful justification, since we have for our Restorer, for our Father, and for our Brother the same Lord who justified Paul; and He is not less powerful nor less holy for us, than for saint Paul."

Chapter 7

A HIDDEN ADVERSARY

Mary as Mother of the Church inspired Ven. Mary of Agreda to reveal a hidden danger, telling how Satan and his demons never cease their wicked activities against the human race. They are constantly planning and devising ways to draw all mankind to join them in their place of eternal torments. Words of Holy Scripture tell us: "Be sober and watch, because your adversary the devil goes about like a roaring lion, seeking whom he may devour." (St. Paul)

The devils begin their work at the moment of conception. They investigate the parents to see if they were guilty of any imperfections in the generating act. They study the child's humors and temperaments; they follow him in his activities, knowing his imperfections and times of greatest danger.

Mary tells us: "The most effective arms against the malign spirits are the divine truths and mysteries of the Divinity and of the most Holy Trinity, of Christ the Savior, of the hypostatic union of the Redemption, and of the immense love with which the Lord as God and man, seeks our eternal salvation; likewise the holiness and purity of most holy Mary, her mysteries and merits, all are presented in new aspects to the vision of the demons so that they are forced to understand and take notice of them through the activity of the holy angels and of God himself."

These truths presented to the demons terrify and torment them so much, they take refuge in the deepest hell.

In addition to all the powerful ministries of the angels, the holy Mother of God uses her majestic powers to defend the souls from all the perils planned and brought about by the activities of the evil spirits. They are constantly defeated by Mary's intervention for the salvation of mankind.

With the conversion of St. Paul, the fallen angels were filled with new fury and Satan held a council to plan a new great persecution against the followers of our Redeemer.

"At the very instant that Our Lord appeared to St. Paul, the devils who were with him to Damascus were hurled to the depths of hell and lay lifeless there until Divinity gave them power to pursue their wickedness again." Some of Satan's thoughts are quoted:

"How is it possible to rest, when every day I see new injuries heaped upon me by this incarnate Word and by the Woman who conceived and bore Him as man? Where is my strength? Where is my power, and of what use is my fury? . . . Saul was our friend, a willing instrument of my designs, subject to my will and command, an enemy of the Crucified, and I had destined him for most cruel torments in this hell . . . Was he not in my service offending God? . . . This example of God's mighty defense of the Church, at the time when I attempted to destroy it through Saul, will draw all the world to his service. Is it possible that I shall see vile humankind raised to the grace and happiness which I have lost, and that it should occupy the heaven from which I have been hurled? This thought torments me more furiously than the fires of hell. I am filled with a powerless rage against myself for not being able to destroy myself in my wrath. But since this is not to be, tell me, my vassals, what shall we do against this so powerful God? . . . and since my majesty is most offended against this Woman, our Enemy, who gave him human being, I wish to inaugurate new ways of destroying her and avenging ourselves for having robbed us of Saul and cast us into the abysses. I shall not rest until I shall have vanquished her. For this purpose I resolve to execute all the plans formed against God and man after my fall from heaven. Come all of you, to help me in my designs and to execute my will." The demons pledged their loyalty and again roamed the world to persecute the fervent Christians.

Words from our Lady to Mary of Agreda:

"My daughter, by no power of human words will you in this mortal life ever succeed in describing the envy of Lucifer and his demons against men, or the malice, astuteness, deceits and ruses, with which in his wrath he seeks to bring them into sin and later on to the eternal torments. He tries to hinder all good works, and such as are performed he tries to minimize, or to destroy and pervert as to their merits. All the malice of which his own mind is capable, he attempts to inject into the souls. Against these attacks God provides admirable protection if men will only co-operate and correspond on their part."

> Blessed is the man who endures temptation,
> for when he has been tried, he will receive
> the crown of life which God has promised to
> those who love Him (James 1:12).

Chapter 8

DAUGHTER, MOTHER, AND SPOUSE

The Holy Trinity looked upon Mary as these three words express. Daughter of the Father, our Creator; Mother of the Son, our Redeemer; and Spouse of the Holy Spirit, the Sanctifier.

Unknown to Satan, our Lady was given the knowledge of his plans to put an end to the followers of Jesus. She pleaded more fervently than ever for divine assistance, offering herself in love to bear all sufferings necessary for the salvation of all human souls. "She understood also, that the Lord portioned out to the Apostles and the faithful that kind of suffering or martyrdom, which corresponded with each one's grace and strength of soul."

Many times, in her loving petitions, Mary, in all her humility, was raised to the highest heaven to enjoy the supreme delight of being seated on a throne next to that of her divine Son. Also many times, Jesus, with beautiful angels came to her oratory in the Cenacle, bringing her consolation and joy, assuring her that all her requests will forever be answered according to her desires.

Mary knew that James would be the first Apostle to begin his appointed ministry, bringing the seeds of Christianity to other parts of the world, especially to the cities of Spain, Italy and Asia Minor. Divinity gave her the knowledge that James would be the first of the Apostles to die as a martyr.

The following words are quoted: "The blessed Lady loved James with special tenderness, and she manifested it in extraordinary favors, conferred upon him during his life until his martyrdom. Saint James deserved these favors on account of his special piety and affection toward Mary, distinguishing himself therein from all the rest. He needed the protection of the great Queen, because he was of a generous and magnanimous heart, and of a most fervent spirit, being resistlessly drawn on to offer himself for labors and dangers. . . . While on his missionary journeys he was indeed like the lightning flash, like the son of thunder, as he was called and designated by his brethren upon entering into the apostolate."

Saint James had preached in Judea for a short time and then proceeded to Carthagena and to Granada. Many times Jesus and Mary sent angels to defend him and to carry him from one region to another in his missionary journeys.

In Granada the unbelieving Jews wished to assassinate James and the twelve disciples whom he had chosen in imitation of his Master. James and his companions were seized and led beyond the city walls, being bound and chained where their captors planned to decapitate them immediately. James prayed as follows to Jesus and Mary: "If it is the will of the Most High, that we here give our lives for the glory of his holy name, do you ask, O Lady, that my soul may be received in his presence. . . . Receive in sacrifice my resignation to the misfortune of not seeing you, if this is to be the last day of my life. O Mary! O Mary!"

Mary had a desire to be with her Apostle, but she did not express this wish to God. However, Jesus then commanded the thousand angels of Mary's guard to carry her on a throne in a beautiful cloud to the place where James and his companions were awaiting martyrdom. The Queen of heaven pronounced these words: "James, my son and dearest friend of my Lord Jesus Christ, be of good heart and be blessed eternally by Him who called and brought you to his divine light. Rise then faithful servant of the Most High, and be free of your bonds."

At these words of Mary, James and his disciples found themselves freed from their chains and realized the time for their martyrdom had not yet come. Their captors who stood with drawn weapons, fell to the earth, remaining for several hours deprived of their senses. The demons who had influenced these persecutors were hurled into the depths of hell, once again being conquered by the powerful Virgin and Queen. James had been the only one who saw the Virgin Mary, but his companions were given an understanding of the miracle and were confirmed in faith, hope and devotion toward the Queen of the Angels.

It was the desire of our powerful Queen that all of Spain should benefit from the preaching and instructions of James. She gave her angels the commands to be with him for guidance and protection as he traversed all the Spanish provinces. In Granada he left some of his disciples who afterwards suffered martyrdom. Then his missionary tours continued in many parts of Andalusia, in Toledo, Portugal Galicia and Asturia. Other places of his ministry were in Rioja, Lograno, Tudela and Saragossa. He left disciples as bishops in different cities of Spain, planting the faith and divine worship. Ven. Mary writes: "The fruit of his preaching in Spain was immense in proportion to the shortness of his stay; and it would be a great error to say or think, that the conversions he made were few."

The schemes of Lucifer were well planned. Each group of demons was given special duties to afflict the members of the Church with the most effective temptations. He brought with him from hell more than two thirds of his demons for this enterprise and left in hell the rest in the depths for the further torture of the damned souls already there.

"The Most High has never permitted full sway to their

envy, for in one moment they would overturn and destroy the whole world; but He gave them a limited freedom, in order that by affliction the Church might take deep roots in the blood and the merits of the saints and so that in persecution and torments might be manifested the wisdom and power of the Pilot directing this little ship of the Church."

With the information gathered by the selected demons, Satan learned about all those with their human weaknesses who had accepted the truths of Christianity.

"Lucifer also pointed out to his demons unbelieving, perfidious, evilminded and depraved men, whom they were to excite and provoke to envious wrath against the followers of Christ. Among these were Herod and many Jews, who abhorred the Crucified and wished to blot out his very name from the land of the living."

For a time the early Church had enjoyed peace, fervor and tranquility. This brought deeper envy and malice to the demons in hell. A great plan for a new persecution was beginning, and Mary saw all the dangers that would happen in Jerusalem. On her countenance was an appearance of sorrow noticed by John. Mary explained the reason, and John showed his concern and care by suggesting they leave this place of danger. Ephesus was chosen as the city to which they would go. He would arrange for their transportation on a ship as soon as possible.

Then happened something which must have come as a surprise to our model of humility. On one of the days before leaving Jerusalem, Mary experienced another special visit from her divine son. He was seated on a throne of glorious majesty surrounded by angels of heavenly beauty in all the choirs and hierarchies. "Then the Lord spoke to her saying, 'My most beloved Mother, of whom I have received human being for the salvation of the world, I am attentive to your petitions and holy desires and they are pleasing to Me. I shall defend my Apostles and my

Church, and I shall be their Father and Protector, so that it shall not be overcome nor the gates of hell prevail against it.' "

Jesus told her it was his desire that she go to Saragossa where the Apostle James was to build a temple in her honor. This was a special favor for the country of Spain. Our Lady prayed: "Grant me, my Son, that in the temple You command to be built by your servant James, I may be permitted to promise the special protection of your almighty arm, and that this sacred place shall be part of my inheritance for the use of all those that call with devotion upon your holy name and ask me to intercede for them with your clemency."

"Christ our Redeemer answered Her: 'My Mother, in whom I am well pleased, I give you my royal word, that I shall look with especial clemency and fill with blessings all those who with devotion and humility call upon Me through your intercession in that temple.' "

"Then at the command of the Lord, a great number of the angels that accompanied Her formed a royal throne of a most resplendent cloud and placed Her thereon as the Queen and Mistress of all creation. Christ the Savior gave them his blessing and ascended with the rest of the angels to heaven."

As they traveled, the holy angels sang hymns in wonderful harmony. James and his companions heard the angelic music. About midnight they arrived in Saragossa and awakened James and his companions. They saw a brilliant light in the sky which seemed like a large luminous globe. They felt an interior joy and sweetness, letting them know a miraculous experience was soon to happen.

"The angels bore with them a small column hewn of marble or jasper; and a not very large image of their Queen made of some other material. This image was carried by the angels with great veneration."

Seated on the heavenly throne, Mary said to the Apostle: "My Son James, this place the most high and omnipotent God of heaven has destined to be consecrated by you upon earth for the erection of a temple and house of prayer, where, under my patronage and name He wishes to be glorified and magnified, where the treasures of his right hand shall be distributed, and all his ancient mercies shall be opened up for the faithful through my intercession, if they ask for them in true faith and sincere piety."

Before leaving, Our Lady said: "You shall immediately begin to build this temple of God, and after you have completed it, you shall depart for Jerusalem; for my divine Son wishes you to offer the sacrifice of your life in the same place where He offered his for the salvation of the human race."

At their Queen's command, the angels carried their beautiful Mistress back to Jerusalem where she made preparations for her voyage to Ephesus.

The temple was built and the shrine was known as "Our Lady of the Pillar." At the time of Ven. Mary of Agreda's revelations in the seventeenth century, it had continued to be in existence.

Chapter 9

LIFE IN EPHESUS

Some of the Christians had come from Jerusalem. As soon as they knew that Mary was in the city, they came to welcome her and offered their dwellings and possessions for her use. Our Queen chose to live in the house where a few retired and poor women were living by themselves, free from intercourse with men. Mary and John gratefully resided there during their stay in Ephesus, where they remained for two and a half years.

John began to preach in the city and made many converts, baptizing them, and strengthening their faith with many miracles. He also had the aid of Mary, who could read their interior inclinations and could speak to the heart of each.

"She wrought prodigies and miracles for the benefit of the unfortunate, curing the possessed and the infirm, succored the poor and the needy, and by the labor of her own hands gave assistance to the sick in the infirmaries, attending upon them in person." Again the fury of Satan was renewed in hatred for the woman who could not be influenced by him to abandon her invincible holiness.

Mary's tender heart was deeply troubled when she thought of the great and magnificent temple dedicated to Diana. This was the place occupied by false virgins under the power of the demons. They were called Amazons, having come from Scythia to Asia Minor — being proud, vainglorious, and warlike. They had made Ephesus the center of their power. One had made herself a goddess called Diana, having beauty, nobility, high intellect and

213

other allurements. Mary's prayers went up to heaven: "Lord God, Most High, worthy of all reverence and praise! It is proper that these abominations, which have lasted for so many years, should cease. My heart cannot bear to see that an unhappy and abominable woman receive the worship due to the true God, such as You alone as the Infinite deserve; nor can I endure to see the name of chastity so profaned and prostituted in honor of the demons."

Our Lord replied: "My Mother, moderate your sorrow and ask whatever you wish; for I shall grant it all and you shall find grace in my eyes to obtain it. I desire that you act according to your wishes, using the power I have given you; do or undo whatever is necessary for the welfare of my Church, and you may be sure that all the fury of the demons will be turned toward you." At Mary's command an angel destroyed the temple, not leaving a stone upon a stone. According to the wishes of Jesus and Mary, nine women were led to safety and repentance. The others lost their lives in the ruins of the building.

Mary was given the grace to know that the Apostle James had arrived in Jerusalem. His preaching incurred the further hatred of Herod and the demons.

An angel said to Mary, "Empress of heaven and our Lady, the most high Lord and God bids you immediately to hasten to Jerusalem to console his great servant James, to assist him in his death and to grant all his loving and holy desires." Then angels carried Mary to the place where the martyrdom of James was taking place. James prayed: "Mother of my Lord Jesus Christ, my Mistress and Protectress, consolation of the afflicted and refuge of the needy, in this hour bestow upon me, my Lady, your so much desired blessing. Offer for me to your Son and Redeemer of the world, the sacrifice of my life, since I am burning with desire to be a holocaust for the glory of his name. Let today your most pure and spotless hands be the altar of my sacrifice, in order that it may become acceptable in the eyes of Him, who died for me upon the cross. Into your hands and through them into the hands of my Creator, I commend my spirit." Mary encouraged him with wonderful consoling words, and when the executioners had beheaded the valiant Apostle, Mary carried his soul to the eternal joys of heaven. An angel had taken her place in Ephesus during her absence. The Apostle's disciples took his body to Galicia in Spain during the following night.

Another benefit of Mary's presence in Ephesus was her influence on a group of devout women who followed her teachings and became like a religious community of today.

In the meantime, Herod had died in a miserable way, and the persecution in Jerusalem was not as severe as it had been. Peter, as head of the Church, convoked a Council, requesting that Mary and John should be present. Many people in Ephesus were sad to see them leave.

Chapter 10

IMPORTANT DECISIONS

The Council was held in the Cenacle where they had met so many times before. Among those attending were Paul and Barnaby. This was the first time that Paul had seen Mary. With tears he told her how sorry he was and asked forgiveness for persecuting her divine Son and Lord. Mary said these sweet words, "Paul, servant of the Most High, if He who created and redeemed you, deigned to call you to his friendship and made you a vessel of election, how can I, his slave, refuse to pardon you."

The procedures of the meeting began with words from Peter, "My Brethren and children in Christ our Savior, it was necessary that we meet in order to solve the difficulties and decide upon the affairs, which our most beloved brethren Paul and Barnaby have brought to our notice, and to determine other matters touching the increase of the holy faith. For thus it is proper that we engage in prayer to obtain the assistance of the Holy Spirit and we shall persevere therein for ten days as is our custom. On the first and on the last days we shall celebrate the sacrifice of the Mass, by which we shall dispose our hearts to receive the divine light."

Mary prepared the hall, cleaning and decorating it with her own hands for the first Mass to be offered the following day. Saint Peter was the celebrant. After Holy Communion on this day of the first Mass, many angels descended to the Cenacle and were seen by all those present. The hall was filled with a wonderful light and fragrance, bringing marvelous effects in their souls. Plans were made for their times of prayer during the following days.

The Mass was again offered on the tenth day with the petition that all present would be enlightened by the coming of the Holy Spirit in his powerful graces.

"Saint Peter, as the head and the highpriest, spoke first, then Paul and Barnaby, and James the Less. . . . The first decision of this Council was that the exact law of the circumcision and the Law of Moses should not be imposed upon the baptized; since eternal salvation was given through Baptism and faith in Christ."

The time was opportune for the writing of the Gospels under the care of Mary. "Saint Peter had already consulted with the Mother of Wisdom, and all the Council having approved of his proposal, they called upon the Holy Spirit to point out the Apostles and disciples who should write the life of the Savior. Immediately a light was seen descending upon Peter and a voice was heard saying: 'The highpriest and head of the Church shall assign four for recording the works and the teachings of the Savior of the world.'" Peter and all present prostrated themselves, giving thanks to the Lord for this favor. When all had again risen, Peter spoke:

"Matthew, our beloved brother, shall immediately begin to write his Gospel, in the name of the Father, the Son and the Holy Spirit. Mark shall be the second, who shall likewise write the Gospel, in the name of the Father, the Son and the Holy Spirit. Luke shall write the third, in the name of the Father, the Son and the Holy Spirit. Our most beloved John shall be the fourth and last to write the mysteries of our Savior and Teacher in the name of the Father, the Son, and the Holy Spirit." This decision the Lord confirmed by permitting the heavenly light to remain until these words were repeated and formally accepted by those appointed.

In a few days Matthew was praying for enlightenment

and Our Lady appeared to him on a glorious throne. He was told to write only what would explain the Incarnation and other mysteries of the Word, making no mention of the glorious mysteries of her own life. After the faith was firmly established in the Church, someone else would write about Mary's own special life, graces and merits. Matthew finished his writing in Judea. He used the Hebrew language in the year 42 of Our Lord.

Four years later, the Evangelist Mark wrote his Gospel while in Palestine. He also wrote in the Hebrew language. While praying for divine enlightenment, Mary appeared to him and said: "The Most High whom you serve and love, sends me to assure you, that your prayers are heard and that his Holy Spirit shall direct you in the writing of the gospel, with which He has charged you." As she had told Matthew, she also told Mark to write nothing about her own gifts and mysteries. At that time our Lady was sixty-one years of age. "St. Jerome says that Mark wrote his short Gospel in Rome, at the instance of the faithful residents there; but I wish to call attention to the fact, that this was a translation or copy of the one he had written in Palestine; for the Christians in Rome possessed neither his nor any other Gospel, and therefore he set about writing one in the Roman or Latin language."

Two years later, Luke wrote his Gospel in the Greek language. Mary appeared to him in Achaia as she had appeared to the two preceding writers. However, Luke was permitted to write what was desirable at that time about Mary's privileges concerning her part in the happenings of the Incarnation and Redemption.

The last of the Evangelists to write his Gospel was John, who wrote in the Greek language during his stay in Asia Minor. This was in the 58th year of the Lord, after the transition of Holy Mary.

"Such were the beginnings of the sacred Gospels, all of them having been commenced with the assistance and by the intervention of the most blessed Mary, giving the Church to understand, that all these benefits have been vouchsafed at her hands."

Chapter 11

LAST YEARS OF MARY'S FAITHFUL PILGRIMAGE

Mary continued her care of the Apostles as a true spiritual mother. Angels were always ready to serve her in any way she wished. Sometimes they carried her to an Apostle who was in need of her wisdom and protective guidance. At other times an Apostle might be transported by the angels to the presence of our powerful Queen, who could solve all their difficulties when her sincere prayers were answered by God. It was her desire that all of them be clothed in the same type of garments worn by our Savior on earth. These she always provided with the help of the angels when needed.

Mary's spiritual graces and merits continued to grow in the sight of God, making her more and more filled with Divinity. If all the special graces of all the saints and angels in heaven were put together, they could never come close to equaling the beauty and joy of the graces given to the humble Mary.

"The most holy Mary had arrived at the age of sixty-seven years without having tarried in her career, ceased in her flight, mitigated the flame of her love, or lessened the increase of her merits from the first instant of her Conception. As all this had continued to grow in each moment of her life, the ineffable gifts, benefits and favors of the Lord had made her entirely godlike and spiritual."

The custom of observing the Church's feast days throughout the year was begun by our Queen. The Passion of Christ was always very vivid in her mind. Mary would remain alone in her oratory from five o'clock on Thursday till noon on Sunday. "Many times she wept tears of blood, which covered her whole face... Sometimes her heart was wrenched from its normal position by the violence of her grief; and when she was in such extremes, her divine Son came from heaven, furnishing her with new strength and life to soothe her sorrow and heal the wounds caused by love of Him, and in order that by such assistance and comfort, she might continue the exercises of her compassion." Saint John or an angel would be taking her place for necessary transactions with others.

"In accordance with the pleasure of the eternal Father, Christ our Savior decreed and as it were pledged Himself to his most blessed Mother, in the presence of all the saints, that from henceforth, as long as She should live in mortal flesh, She should on every Sunday after finishing her exercises of the Passion, be brought by the holy angels to the empyrean heaven and there, in the presence of the Most High, celebrate in body and soul the joys of the Resurrection. The Lord also decreed, that in her daily Communion He should manifest to Her his most sacred humanity united to the Divinity in a new and wonderful manner, different from that in which She had enjoyed it until that day; so that this might serve as a pledge and foretaste of the glory, which He had reserved for his most holy Mother in eternity."

Other feasts which Mary observed in an appropriate way were the Incarnation and Nativity, Circumcision, Adoration of the Kings, Purification, Baptism of the Lord, his fast, institution of the Blessed Sacrament, Resurrection, the Ascension of Christ and the coming of the Holy Spirit, and also her own Immaculate Conception, Birthday and Purification.

One day the archangel Gabriel surrounded by other celestial spirits entered the oratory of the Blessed Virgin, letting her know when her mortal life would be changed to that of eternity. With heavenly grace he said: "Our Empress and Lady, the Omnipotent and the Holy of the holy sends us from his heavenly court to announce to You in his name the most happy end of your pilgrimage and banishment upon earth in mortal life. Soon, O Lady, is that day and hour approaching, in which, according to your longing desires, You shall pass through natural death to the possession of the eternal and immortal life, which awaits You in the glory and at the right hand of your divine Son, our God. Exactly three years from today You shall be taken up and received into the everlasting joy of the Lord, where all its inhabitants await You, longing for your presence." Mary answered in the same words as at the Incarnation of the Word: "Behold the handmaid of the Lord; Be it done according to your word."

The day for Mary's joyful transition to the heavenly mansions had arrived. Through the providence of God, the Apostles and disciples were gathered in the Cenacle where they found Mary in her oratory, kneeling on her couch in prayer. Peter and John were the first to enter, followed by the other Apostles, then Paul and disciples. They knew this was the last day that their treasure of goodness would be with them. This was a loss so great that they were in tears of grief. To see them in such sadness made Mary tearful also. With great reverence, Mary asked for their blessings and promised to always keep them in her heart. Then she reclined on her couch and celestial music was heard.

"Mary pronounced these words of her Son on the Cross: 'Into thy hands, O Lord, I commend my spirit.' Then she closed her virginal eyes and expired. The sickness which took away her life was love without any other weakness or accidental intervention of whatever kind."

"A divine fragrance was spread about, which penetrated even to the street." This happened at three o'clock on Friday, the same hour in which our Savior had died on the

Cross. It was the thirteenth day of August, in Mary's seventieth year of age.

There was a short discussion about the burial duties. It was decided that the two maidens who had been so helpful to Mary should prepare her body in the usual manner. When they entered the room there was such a refulgence coming from Mary's body, that they were blinded and could not even see the particular place where it lay. In great excitement they told the Apostles what had happened. Peter and John then entered the oratory and prayed for enlightenment. Words were heard: "Let not the sacred body be uncovered or touched." The refulgence had diminished somewhat, and they brought a bier. Then Peter and John held the tunic at the two ends and placed it on the bier, feeling no weight from the body as they did so.

A procession was formed to take the body of Mary to a sepulcher in the Valley of Josephat. Many miracles happened as the angelic music and the wonderful fragrance continued. There were thousands of angels, the Apostles and disciples, and most of the inhabitants of Jerusalem. Many of the sick were cured, many possessed were freed from the demons, and there were miraculous conversions among the Jews and gentiles, asking for Baptism.

With joyful reverence John and Peter placed the celestial Treasure in the sepulcher and covered it with a linen cloth. A large stone was placed at the entrance as in other burials. It was agreed that some of the disciples should be on watch at the tomb as long as the music continued. The most pure soul of Mary was taken up to heaven with great jubilation as the angels and saints awaited all further glory to come. It was the desire of God that Mary should return on the third day to resuscitate her sacred body and unite herself with it so that she might again be raised to the right hand of her divine Son.

On the third day at midnight, exactly at the time of the

Resurrection of Our Lord, Mary, in body and soul, with a glorious procession of angels was taken up to heaven.

A final quote from Ven. Mary of Agreda's writing: "The three divine Persons placed upon the head of the most blessed Mary a crown of such new splender and value, that the like has been seen neither before or after by any mere creature. At the same time a voice sounded from the throne saying: 'My beloved, chosen among the creatures, our kingdom is yours; You shall be the Lady and Sovereign of the seraphim, of all the ministering spirits, the angels and of the entire universe of creatures. Attend, proceed and govern prosperously over them, for in our supreme consistory we give You power, majesty and sovereignty, being filled with grace beyond all the rest. . . . nothing do We wish to be given to the world, which does not pass through your hands; and nothing do we deny, which You wish to concede to men. Grace shall be diffused in your lips for obtaining all that You wish and ordained in heaven and on earth, and everywhere shall angels and men obey You; because whatever is ours shall be yours, just as You have always been ours; and You shall reign with Us forever.'"

FOR APPROBATIONS, NOTICES, INTRODUCTIONS

Please refer to:

1. The Divine Life of the Most Holy Virgin,
                    TAN Books and Publishers, Inc.
                    Rockford, Illinois 61105
   Being an Abridgement of The Mystical City of God
   by Ven. Mary of Agreda, Abridged by Fr. Bonaventure Amedeo de Caesavea, MC

2. A Popular Abridgement of   TAN Books
   The Mystical City of God

3. The Four Volume   Ava Maria Institute
   The Mystical City of God by Ven. Mary of Agreda
   Translated from the original Spanish by Fiscar
   Marison (begun in 1902)

4. The Life of Ven. Mary of Agreda
                    Republished by Alex J. Fiato and
                    Leonard M. Sieradski
                    Reprinted by: Mary's Helpers, Inc.
                    Marrero Louisiana, 2002

5. Wisdom the Woman   Published by Sir Knights
   According to Agreda   Alex J. Fiato and
   by James A. Carrico   Leonard M. Sieradski

6. The Life of Mary   TAN Books
   As Seen by the Mystics
   Compiled by Raphael Brown
   Reference Particulary To:
   Foreword
   Introduction
   Bibliography
   Supplement To Bibliography (As of 1975)

7. The Age of Mary, January - February 1958
                              Our Lady of Sorrows
   Province of the Order of Servants of Mary (Servites)
                              3121 West Jackson Blvd.
                              Chicago, Illinois 60612

A copy of this historical study of Venerable Mary of
Agreda and her "Mystical City of God" is available at
the above Province office for perusal and study with prior
written approval of the Province.

A copy is also available at:
Archangel Gabriel Enterprises, Inc. ©
37137 Butternut Ridge Road
Elyria, OH 44035
440.327.4532

AUTHORS AND PUBLISHERS

Who have been of especial help

John M. Haffert
Stephen Foglien
Dr. Rosalie A. Turton
Thomas A. Nelson
Minuteman Press, Inc., Canton, Massachusetts
I-Supply, Galway, Ireland
Rev. Peter Mary Rookey, O.S.M.
Rev. Amideus Mary Wickers, O.S.M.
Rev. Conrad Borntrager, O.S.M.
Apostleship of Prayer, Milwaukee, WI

Appendix C

CURRENT CANONICAL EXPLANATION

Response to Apparitions and Visionaries
for Roman Catholics

Since the abolition of Canon 1399 and 2318 of the former Code of Canon Law by Paul VI in AAS58 (1966) page 1186, publications about new apparitions, revelation, prophecies, miracles, etc., have been allowed to be distributed and read by the faithful without the express permission of the Church, providing that they contain nothing which contravenes faith and morals. This means, no imprimatur is necessary.

The Discernment of Visionaries and Apparitions Today
By Albert J. Hebert, S.M., Page III

Special Thanks to:
Apostleship of Prayer
3211 S. Lake Drive, Suite 216
Milwaukee, WI 53235
www.apostlesofprayer.org

Distributed by:

Archangel Gabriel Enterprises, Inc.©
37137 Butternut Ridge Road
Elyria, OH 44035
440-327-8006
http://www.holylove.org